PAUL TILLICH:

A THEOLOGY FOR THE

21ST CENTURY

PAUL TILLICH:

A THEOLOGY FOR THE

21ST CENTURY

Richard M. Pomeroy

Hope you guys read this
closely. I think you would
find it interesting.
from who you would

Grandpa Pomeroy

Writer's Showcase
San Jose New York Lincoln Shanghai

PAUL TILLICH: a theology for the 21st century

Writer's Showcase
an imprint of iUniverse, Inc.

For information address:
iUniverse, Inc.
5220 S. 16th St., Suite 200
Lincoln, NE 68512
www.iuniverse.com

ISBN: 0-595-21109-7

Printed in the United States of America

CONTENTS

CHAPTER 1

Existence: God And The Search For Christ

CHAPTER 2

Finding The Christ: What Then?

CHAPTER 3

The Uncertainties Of Life: The Search For Security

REALIZING ONE'S POTENTIAL THROUGH SELF-INTEGRATION SELF-CREATIVITY, AND SELF-TRANSCENDENCE

THE SEARCH FOR A LIFE FREE OF PROBLEMS

CHAPTER 4

The Divine Spirit

CHAPTER 5

Life And The Divine Spirit

CHAPTER 6

The Trinity

CHAPTER 7

History And The Search For The Kingdom Of God

CHAPTER 8

The Kingdom Of God Within History

CHAPTER 9

The Kingdom Of God And The End Of History

PREFACE

I was a full time seminary student within weeks of my retirement from the U.S. Forest Service after a 31 year career. I retired on my 55th birthday, anxious to begin seminary in search of the meaning behind the numerous, sometimes miraculous experiences I encountered during my life. I found what I was looking for in the *Systematic Theology* of Paul Tillich.

My career began as a field forester in NW Washington State, later as a District Forest Ranger, responsible for the management of some 200,000 acres of land, as a Fire Boss on some of the largest conflagrations in the West, as a director of a Job Corps Conservation Center, and as an Assistant Regional Forester and director of personnel for the U.S. Forest Service in California and Hawaii with its 10,000 employees.

This is not the place to relate all of the experiences which provided me the motivation to attend seminary. One experience is worthy of relating in some detail, however, as it had a major impact on me, my values, and the direction that my life has taken. During the War On Poverty of President Johnson's Administration I was given the opportunity to become the director of a Job Corps Center near Roseburg, Oregon, one of the first centers to open nationally.

The Job Corps program involved the establishment of residential living centers designed to teach disadvantaged youth how to read, write, add, subtract, divide, and even do a little algebra. Establishing a discipline of work as well as cultivating skills needed in the job market were also important parts of the program. We were to break the cycle of poverty in which the corpsmen were entrapped and in which, in most instances, many generations of their families had existed. We were to do all of this

with approximately 225 corpsmen at a time in each of the larger con-
servation centers. Three out of four corpsmen could not read or write
when they arrived. Many of these young men had been involved in the
burning of the inner-cities of Detroit and Chicago, in Harlem and in
Watts during the riots of the 1960s. Today, they would be the Bloods
and Crips, the neighborhood gangs of the inner cities...suffice it to say,
I discovered miracles within these young men as they developed their
potential in the Job Corps, no matter the poor circumstances under
which many of them had been raised...Miracles of human develop-
ment literally sprang from these efforts, providing me with an aware-
ness that yes, anything is possible through an application of love and
care, mixed with some good down-to-earth work and counsel. I began
to experience the goodness in people...A corpsmen received his first
award ever—he became a "polliwog"—because he was able to stay
afloat for one minute in a swimming pool. Within three months follow-
ing this small success he had learned to read and write at the eighth-
grade level...Written material was prepared by one of the staff, an
ex-logger, on how to use and maintain a power saw; this was done
completely on his own time and initiative without any thought of pay
or reward...corpsmen firefighting crews working for little or no pay,
satisfied at doing a job that needed to be done, wives of Job Corps staff
sewing buttons on corpsmen's shirts, working as volunteers, rewarded
by the tears in the corpsmen's eyes, because no one had ever bothered to
sew a button on their shirt before.[1]

---

[1]. Richard Pomeroy, *In Search of Meaning* (Berkeley: Glen Berkeley Press, 1991),
pp. 6-7, 17. This is a series of reflections that applies parts of Tillich's theology to real
life experiences and values.

It was these kinds of experiences—plus many more of them during my days as a forester, firefighter, director of personnel, and husband/father—which brought me into seminary, searching for the mystery behind it all. I had seen miracles, experienced new values and insights that made my former career advancement goals seemingly unimportant. Unknowingly, I had discovered Tillich's transcendent God through the many roles I had played in my life.

While a seminary student, I had the opportunity to spend most of one year studying Paul Tillich's three volumes on *Systematic Theology*. Up until this time I knew nothing of Tillich and less about his theology. I found it exceedingly difficult to understand and found it necessary to outline many of his paragraphs and chapters in order to gain some comprehension of what he was saying. This served me well as I participated in weekly seminars led by Durwood Foster, Professor of Theology, at the Pacific School of Religion.

Though I gained from all of my studies in seminary, the seminars on Paul Tillich's theology had a special meaning for me as each seminar addressed issues or experiences within my life. For the first time I began to gain insights regarding my journey of faith, a strong faith, but one that I had difficulty understanding and talking about. The miracles at work, the miraculous experiences that I had experienced through much of my life, as a "War On Poverty" Job Corps Director, as a Personnel Director, and subsequently as a Peace Corps volunteer, began to make sense.

I graduated from seminary in 1984, determined that I would make Tillich's theology available to a much broader audience than found within the walls of a seminary. This has become something of an obsession with me as I committed myself to writing an interpretation of Tillich's *Systematic Theology* that could be read, understood and valued by all of us. I reasoned that if it has so much meaning for me, surely it would have the same or similar value for others

Though there have been many people who have contributed to the writing of this book, I have been actively assisted in the last year by a number of "editors" that have materially assisted me in preparing this final version of *PAUL TILLICH: a theology for the 21st century.* Olive my wife of 48 years has not only helped me with the editing but has served as a source of encouragement in my efforts, though I suspect that she is a little full of Tillichian thought. She is forever patient with me, however. Carol Kent and Jane Rhodes have also been of great help, each one addressing my manuscript from somewhat of a different perspective. Jack Williams, an ex-Forest Service cohort, and Harlow Lennon, one of my Portland friends, provided me something of a skeptics view of Tillich's theology and my ability to interpret it. Their "feedback" was not always comfortable. And of particular importance, is the work of Al Leonard who volunteered to help (after I asked him), and who with great patience, and with great editing skill, provided me a paragraph by paragraph critique that resulted in significant improvements.

Richard Pomeroy
November 2001

INTRODUCTION

The intent of the introduction is to help the reader better understand some of the principal thought of Paul Tillich before reading the entire text. Though this interpretation of Tillich's theology is materially easier to read and understand than his original text, his theology continues to be sufficiently complex that an understanding of his principal theological thought will help materially.

Tillich's approach to theology—Of great importance to Tillich, is a theology that is relevant to the human condition as it exists today. His theology begins with the scriptures, however, he borrows heavily from philosophy, history, poetry, and aesthetics, including many of the social and natural sciences in providing this relevancy.

He does not suggest that we abandon past tradition and dogma if it remains relevant to the present. When it serves to stifle thought, however, he believes that it is an impediment to theological progressivism and relevancy. Though valuing tradition his thought is quite modern.

The nature of God/the "ground of being"—God is a God of love, and as such, is the very "ground of being" in Tillich's theology. The ground of being pointing to the mother-quality of giving birth, of nurture, rather than dominance. God, though "...*as the ground of being infinitely transcends that of which he is the ground.*" [2]

God is that from which we spring, the soil "that makes the flower grow," personally sharing in the joys, the sorrows, and the strife experienced in

---

2. Paul Tillich, *Systematic Theology*, Volume II (Chicago: The University of Chicago Press, 1957), pp. 8-9

the world, yet not being limited by them but transcends them. God influences the course of history through the power of his love present in the human spirit. Though God's love is powerful and free to all, it is not controlling. If God controlled everything, God would have to withdraw a precious trust, freedom. He suggests, however, that to do so will require a new and revised understanding of the divine Life and the divine Spirit, including that of male-female symbolism. To this end, Tillich introduces the concept "ground of being" which points to the mother-quality of giving birth, a quality attributed to God.

God's purpose for humanity/Courage to be—"*The courage to be is the ethical act in which man affirms his own being in spite of those elements of his existence which conflict with his essential self-affirmation.*"[3] In other words, God wants one to have the courage to be all that one can possibly be in pursuing one's potential goodness. The power to do this lies in the power of the freedom that God bestowed on humans during the Creation, a freedom to grow toward God or to choose estrangement, or separation from God. Without the freedom to pursue one's essential goodness (Genesis 1:31) and the ability to make decisions for oneself, good or bad, human beings would be nothing but puppets of God.

Myths, symbols and literalism—Tillich believes that symbols and myths are the essential ways of addressing matters of the divine, they are not un-truths. Symbols and myths represent theological truths that

---

[3.] Paul Tillich, *The Courage to Be* (New Haven and London: Yale University Press, 1952), p. 3.

orthodox language is unable to convey with understanding.[4] According to Tillich, no attempt should be made to replace them by a scientific substitute, nor should they be subjected to scientific analysis, as they are the language of faith, not of science.

One of Tillich's major concerns with religion, is the seemingly never ending debate on whether a particular event in the Bible is symbol or "literal truth." The nature of the debate often includes an inference that symbolism and literalism (biblical in errancy) are mutually exclusive. This is nonsense, according to Tillich, and serves to eclipse the value of symbolism whose theological truth is not dependent on literalism.

Tillich does not believe that it is important whether the miracles in the Bible are literally true. He personally questions their basis in fact, as they are contrary to the natural laws of God. He believes that God governs according to natural law and does not unilaterally enter into an event, controlling its outcome. In believing this he admits, however, that he may be wrong.

The New Being—The physical reality of a New Being occurred almost two thousand years ago in Jesus the Christ. The New Being, when present in individual persons, represents a changed reality in the life of the person despite the degree to which the person is estranged (sinful). The New Being spans all of history and existed well before its revelation in Jesus the Christ. Its value and meaning, according to Tillich, does not depend on whatever historical picture New Testament scholarship may produce.

---

4 Paul Tillich, *The Dynamics of Faith* (NY: Harper and Brothers Publishers, 1957), p.51.

Although Jesus manifested himself as the New Being 2000 years ago, the full realization of the Kingdom of God, did not arrive with him—it continues its process of arriving, through the presence of a New Being in the lives of individual believers.

Revelation—Tillich combines the best of traditional values with a human spirit in which God (the divine Spirit) resides. He believes that revelation takes place through God's presence within the spirit of human beings if they are open to hearing. Continuous revelation from God provides the church with the ability to address the problems of freedom and justice within the world and, according to Tillich, an important criteria for recognizing "true revelation" is to ask the question "is the revelation consistent with the great commandments of Jesus?"

You shall love the Lord your God with all your heart, and with all your soul, and with all your mind. This is the great and first commandment. And a second is like it, You shall love your neighbor as yourself. On these two commandments depend all the law and the prophets. (Matthew 22:37-40)

Sin—Tillich tells us that all humans exist in a state of sin (estrangement), and it is rooted in one or a combination of three basic causes: (1) unbelief, (2) hubris, and (3) concupiscence.

Unbelief occurs when people turn away from God, the source of all that is good. Hubris occurs when, in unbelief, one substitutes one's own self for God, exhibiting excessive pride or arrogance. In essence, making oneself God. And concupiscence, occurs when one, working through others, dominates and exploits everything possible, pursuing an unlimited desire for abundance in material possessions, knowledge, power, sex and all other aspects of one's relation to the world.

Paul Tillich-A Biographical Sketch

1886–1965

One of the twentieth century's greatest theologians and philosophers, Paul Tillich spent much of his life integrating traditional Christianity with modern culture. He believed strongly that theology was relevant only when it addressed the meaning of human existence.

Paul Tillich was born in 1886 in the province of Brandenburg, Germany, but raised in Schonfliess, a small community east of the Elbe River. His father was a Lutheran pastor and bishop. He studied in a number of universities, and received a Doctor of Philosophy degree from the University of Breslau and a licentiate in theology from the University of Halle in 1912. During World War I he was a chaplain in the German army where he confronted the issues of war and death. This experience led him to question the relevance of the church as an organized body. Immediately following the war he taught at the Universities of Berlin, Marburg, Dresden, Leipzig and Frankfurt.

Tillich saw himself as both a bourgeois and a bohemian; as a theologian and an academician. As a Bishop's son, he spent much time visiting the manor houses of the very rich yet he ended up a socialist. Although educated in the 19th century classical tradition, his thought was quite modern. He valued the best traditions of the past, though he did not let the past dampen his natural creativity.

Following the war he became a leader of the religious socialist movement in Germany. During this period he wrote essays and articles while participating in many groups searching for a new understanding of the human situation. This was during a period when many of his contemporaries considered the world to be in a cultural breakdown.

When Hitler and the national socialists took over Germany, Tillich heeded the call of another great theologian, Reinhold Neibuhr, to come to America and join the faculty at Union Theological Seminary at Columbia University. He arrived in America at age 47, impoverished, powerless, and uncomfortable with the language and the culture. The timing for his move to the United States, however, could not have been better as Tillich's passionate concern for freedom had made him an early critic of Hitler and the Nazis. Immediately prior to his leaving Germany, Hitler barred him from teaching at German universities. According to Tillich, he was the first non-Jewish academician to be so honored.

He has been described by his biographer, Rollo May, as having an extraordinary charisma. According to May, his lectures had an almost child-like quality of openness, revealing his very being. He mesmerized students and audiences, despite a slow, steady—and at times—ponderous delivery in a thick German accent.

Tillich was in great demand as a speaker and had a large public following which included many people not usually concerned with religious matters. As an example, in 1963 he came to Berkeley to deliver the Earl Lectures at the Pacific School of Religion. While in Berkeley, he also delivered an address at the University of California concerning conflicts between science, religion and philosophy. A record 7,500 students attended.

His mind was amazingly creative and had great breadth and perception, ranging from the analytical to the artistic. He taught at three universities while in the United States, the Union Theological Seminary at Columbia, Harvard, and the University of Chicago. During this time he completed his three volume *Systematic Theology* (1951-1963), considered one of the outstanding works of Protestant theology. In addition to *Systematics* he is best known for *Courage to Be* (1952) and the *Dynamics of Faith* (1957). All of his writing develops themes in aesthetics, metaphysics, philosophical anthropology, social thought and theology.

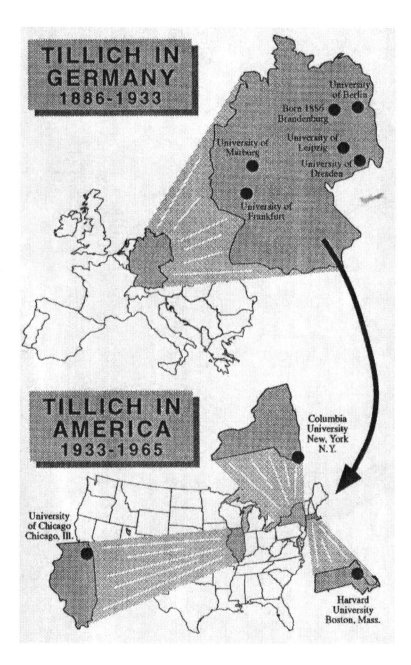

GLOSSARY

atonement: a process which begins when one is enveloped by the New Being in Christ, enabling one to then overcome the past and start a new life in Jesus the Christ.

bondage of the will: the inability of people, no matter how hard they may try, to effect a union with God totally on their own. Only God's love (which is a free and unmerited gift from God to all people), enables one to leave a life of bondage and into a New Being.

Calvinism: involves the practicing of an asceticism of self-discipline, based on a strong moral conviction rather than on a simple rejection of the "world." There is a presumption that all of life is immersed in a "fallen state of reality" within which all temptations must be resisted.

The avoidance of anything that could possibly be construed as sinful, results in a severe asceticism. Often times, areas of denial were petty and ludicrous, such as music, radios, going to movies and the like. According to Tillich, churches, today, have generally gotten over this extreme and distorted Calvinism. It threatens the possibility of living one's life to the fullest and the development of one's full humanity.

concupiscence: occurs when a person dominates and exploits everything possible within life, pursuing an unlimited desire for abundance in material possessions, knowledge, power, sex and all other aspects of one's relation to the world. Along with unbelief and hubris, is one of the three basic causes of sin.

depth psychology: the study of the unconscious

dimensions: the concept of dimensions suggests a hierarchial pyramid which provides Tillich the ability to examine life from a three dimensional standpoint: depth, breadth and height. The concept of dimensions is used to illustrate a basic premise of Tillich's: God's purpose in creating living things is to have them maximize their total potential through the realization of the highest possible attainment in psychological and spiritual development.

essential goodness (nature): according to Tillich, people are essentially good, as was Adam before he took a bite from the forbidden fruit. It is the wish of God that all humans realize their essential goodness as they progress through life.

estrangement: separation from God through acts of unbelief, hubris and concupiscence.

faith: "…the state of being grasped by an ultimate concern…." According to Tillich, faith is continually being confused with belief in something for which there is no evidence, or in something intrinsically unbelievable, or in absurdities and nonsense.

healing: the Greek word "salvus" originally meant "to heal." Tillich believes this meaning is much more appropriate than the commonly understood version of "being saved for eternal life." According to Tillich, it is impossible to separate the idea of salvation from healing, which, theologically, means the reuniting of humans with God, with themselves, and with the entire world. Salvation, as healing, is the very essence of Jesus' ministry to the world.

historical analysis or inquiry: historical research (includes archaeology, literary and form criticism)

historical Jesus—evidence, other than in the scriptures, that Jesus actually lived in the world. According to Tillich, proving the existence of a "historical Jesus" through a search of documents other than the Bible provides a minimum of reliable facts about the man Jesus of Nazareth, and his life. This could lead one to conclude that Jesus did not exist. This is not necessarily so, however.

hubris: the self-elevation of one's self to the level of God. Those who are in a state of hubris do not recognize their own limits and are filled with excessive pride or arrogance, acting as though they are God.

Kingdom of God: it has two aspects to its meaning, one of which is inner-historical (within history) and the other trans-historical (beyond history). Inner-historically, the Kingdom of God is the ultimate aim of history, and is realized through the activity of the divine Spirit. Trans-historically, the Kingdom of God has arrived, and is identical with Eternal Life." (Matthew 6:10).

latent church: Tillich refers to a latent or "hidden" church, as those institutions that are obviously influenced by the divine Spirit and the New Being even though they may be indifferent or even hostile to religion. Examples may include may include educational, artistic, and political movements.

latent Spiritual Community: those who desire to participate in a group whose foundation is the acceptance of Jesus as the Christ, though they may not personally believe in Jesus the Christ.

myth: a traditional story of unknown authorship, ostensibly with a historical basis, usually involving the exploits of gods and heroes.

New Being: a changed reality based on the assumption that humans are basically good despite the degree to which an individual is estranged. The New Being removes an individual from under a law of judgment to an existence in which the law becomes the very essence of the person. The law is internalized within the person and no longer exists as a separate "you shall" or as a law of judgment. A person is, instead, motivated to do that which is "intrinsically right," rather than motivated from a fear of judgment and punishment.

In Christianity, the physical reality of a New Being occurred almost two thousand years ago in Jesus the Christ (the Messiah). Although Jesus manifested himself as the New Being then, the full realization of the Kingdom of God did not arrive with him—it continues its process of arriving through God's continuous revelation today.

"new eon:" a time in which all sin is abolished. During the life of the Apostles it was expected that a New Eon would arrive with a second coming of Christ. Rather than an immediate second coming of Christ and the abolishment of sin, however, the "new eon" came and continues to come within the lives of individual people as a New Being, transforming lives in a manner similar to the Apostles' transformation at Pentecost. The hope of humanity for a "new eon" has been fully realized in Jesus as the Christ, who is the ultimate ideal.

piety: devotion to religious duties and practice.

Protestant ethic: stressed the holiness of one's daily life visible through industriousness, thrifty living, and careful management of material things.

realms: a section of life that contains two or more dimensions, one of which is always dominant. The human realm, as an example, is made up of all dimensions, and is generally thought of as under the dominance of the psychological dimension. The organic realm is made up of both the organic and inorganic dimensions, and in this case the organic dimension is dominant.

regeneration: the power of the divine Spirit (New Being) working within one's life

sacramental: looked at in a broader sense, may include everything in which the divine Spirit has been experienced without limitation on specific types and numbers; i.e., baptism and communion in most of Protestantism,

salvation: See healing

sanctification: the process which moves one's life toward God through faith and love

secular: relating to worldly things rather than religious; not sacred or religious

self-creativity: though it is something of an accelerated version of self-integration, self-creativity is dominated by a drive to become "other than I am." The person in this process is involved in a substantial change from the old self.

self-integration: the process of gaining new experiences, integrating them with all past experiences, resulting in a changed person. It continuously involves growth producing as well as disintegrating experiences, often times occurring at the same time.

self-salvation: trying to overcome one's sinful existence without the love of God and the reality of a New Being

self-transcendence: the process of movement toward God. It cannot be measured as in science, or through direct, observable experiences. It is a matter of one's inner consciousness.

sin: separation from God through acts of unbelief, hubris, and concupiscence.

Spiritual Community: those people, through the experience of the New Being, that are able overcome the ambiguities in religion. Tillich uses the term Spiritual Community rather than Church (although many people in churches are taken up by the New Being), for two reasons: (1) the ambiguities and secularization found in the organized Church, and (2) the Spiritual Community is also found outside the church. The Spiritual Community is hidden, yet very real. It is hidden, however, only in the sense that it cannot be seen, understood, or experienced by those of no faith. This is due to the absence of the New Being in their life.

theonomy: the state of the culture under the impact of the divine Spirit. Included within a theonomous culture is the aim that all humans will develop toward a loving, transcendent God. It is important to note that the aim or direction comes from within theonomy, it is not externally imposed.

There are several characteristics of a theonomous culture deserving special attention. It must, as an example, communicate an experience of holiness, of something ultimate in being and meaning, in all that it does. Another characteristic is the affirmation of one's right to creative self-expression. There is no theonomy where justice is rejected in the name of God, or where an act of self-determination is prevented by a sacred tradition, or where a new style of creative expression is suppressed in the name of some form of absoluteness that rejects the new.

Word of God: Tillich enlarges indefinitely the number of words that can become the Word of God. If they transmit the Spirit of God, all religious and cultural documents, the whole of human literature, even that which is average or small, is the Word of God. The spoken word, in sermon or in ordinary conversation, can also become the Word of God.

The question naturally arises as to how one distinguishes the "true" word of God from the many competing and contradictory words whose proponent's claim they are "the" Word of God? Tillich responds that nothing is the Word of God if it contradicts the faith and love as recorded in the Bible.

CHAPTER 1

Existence: God And The Search For Christ

Chapter Introduction

Much of the essence of Tillich's theology is captured in this chapter which is further developed in the remaining chapters. The major points of Tillich's theology found in this chapter are:

(1) The *Ground of Being*, God, influences the course of history rather than controlling it;

(2) humans are essentially good (Genesis 1:31);

(3) humans enjoy a unique freedom, as God intends, though there is a price to pay for this freedom, sinfulness;

(4) God desires that all humans have the *courage to be* all that they can become, developing to their highest potential, rising above their sinfulness and living a fulfilling life;

(5) love alone, through the power of one's New Being in Christ, provides the power needed to overcome one's sinfulness, providing salvation; and

(6) true religion involves a personal encounter and union with God, through the transforming power of the divine Spirit.

The Nature of God, God's Desire for Humanity: The Gift of Freedom

The nature of God—Basic to Tillich's theology is a God, the source of all being, who *influences* the course of history—rather than controlling it—through the power of love working within the human spirit. God as the source of all being, shares in the joy and sorrow of the human experience, yet transcends the human experience to a sacred realm that Tillich refers to as "ecstatic holiness." This concept of God is not unique with Tillich. Many theologians such as Luther, Zwingli, Calvin and Schleiermacher have accepted this view.

According to Tillich, however, the common theological view of God is of a supernatural being, separate from all other beings; one who created the universe in six days, who has a master plan for the world, and acts to control it, assuring that the master plan is carried out. God, in this view, does not interact personally with humans, but observes the world from a distance, and makes judgments of right and wrong.

God's desire for humanity: the gift of freedom—Having the courage to become all that one can become, the realizing of one's "essential goodness," one's total potential, and the leading of a fulfilling life is what God desires for all human beings, according to Tillich. This can best be understood by considering the gift that God has given humans, the gift of freedom. It is God's purpose that humans will use their freedom to pursue their essential goodness as—"God saw everything he had made and behold it was very good" (Genesis 1:31). If humans did not have the freedom to make decisions for themselves, good or bad, they would be nothing more than puppets of God without individual purpose or mind. They would not be human beings.

And God saw everything that he had made, and behold, it was very good.
(Genesis 1:31)

"Humans are Essentially Good"

Humans, in contrast to all other living things, are free to make choices. They have language with which to express ideas, they can penetrate into deeper and deeper levels of reality, and they can rise above the conditions of the current human situation. They can think and make decisions, and they can modify their behavior from that of pure instinct. In this latter sense, humans, after being provoked, can "turn the other cheek," an ability that no other living thing has developed.

Humans are also free to create technical tools and products to satisfy their needs, create a world of beauty through painting, song or poem, or a world of structure and organization. And of great importance, they can contradict what God would wish them to do as Adam did when he ate the forbidden fruit. Humans can even give up their freedom and allow themselves to be suppressed or dominated. It is this freedom that makes humans uniquely different from all other living creatures. It is this freedom that enables humans to develop toward the ecstatic holiness of God. It is also this freedom that results in the loss of their "innocence," as happened to Adam.

Tillich reminds us that when humans begin to exercise their freedom, they lose their "innocence," as their freedom is conditioned by external-internal forces not totally within the control of the individual. His reasoning is as follows:

1. There is no identifiable time within natural evolution when animal nature (which is not free) was replaced by human nature (which is free). Both natures have been combined within the human, and often devastatingly so.

2. It is uncertain at what point in the life of an individual that sufficient maturity occurs so that one can take full responsibility for one's actions. Legally, it is usually considered to be when one reaches the age of 18 years. This suggests that those under 18 are unduly influenced by animal nature and those over eighteen are not. Lines such as these are not distinct.

3. When one reaches maturity and is theoretically responsible for one's own actions, there are many stages of reduced ability that accompanies the maturity. One is unable to make fully "rational" responses due to tiredness, sickness, intoxication, stress and various mental disorders. These may not remove one's responsibility but do show how an individual's ability to act freely is limited by factors not completely under the person's control.

4. How do the unconscious aspects of a person's being effect conscious decisions? How often do we make decisions without understanding all the motives behind our act?

These are but a few considerations that Tillich discusses concerning the manner in which a person's individual freedom is modified. Biological, psychological and sociological factors are a part of every decision. Humans are not as free as one would initially believe. Despite these multiple influences, it is possible, however, for humans to make decisions consistent with their potential goodness. The decisions of Jesus provide the perfect model for this.

The Price of Freedom: Sinfulness

The nature of sinfulness—Freedom provides one the latitude to do as God would have one do, to live a fulfilling life with God as its center, or to live a life of sinfulness. Never, however, does one totally conquer all of one's sinful ways, according to Tillich. To some degree all people live a sinful life, only Jesus the Christ was able to do otherwise.

According to Tillich, a human being's estranged (sinful) condition occurs through one or more of three basic sins that are the root cause of all other sins. They are the sins of: (1) unbelief, (2) hubris, and (3) concupiscence. *Unbelief*, according to Tillich, occurs when one turns away from God and toward oneself in the realizing of one's freedom. It is not simply the rejection of church doctrine. *Hubris* is the self-elevation of one's self to the level of God. Those who are in a state of hubris, do not recognize their own limits; they are filled with excessive pride or arrogance. They act as though they are God. Finally, *concupiscence* occurs when one working through others, dominates and exploits everything possible, pursuing an unlimited desire for abundance in material possessions, knowledge, power, sex and all other aspects of one's relation to the world.

People become estranged as the result of their own actions. It should be understood, however, that the act was at least in part determined by past conditions beyond their control. Sin and estrangement are usually thought of in individualistic terms. It is the individual person who sins.

It is looked at by some, however, in a collective sense, as an entire group or nation. The idea of collective sin and estrangement have been with us almost from the beginning of civilization. There have always been rulers, nations, movements of one sort or another that have acted in concert against humanity's best interests. This has been accompanied by society's condemnation of associates and descendants of those involved who are innocent. As an example, during and following World War II, the entire nation of Germany was condemned, including those Germans who actively resisted the immorality of the German leadership. This was often done at great risk to themselves.

Condemning innocent members or the descendants of a group is wrong, according to Tillich. He points out a fundamental difference between an individual and a group, or a nation. An individual has one decision maker with a maximum of freedom to act. A group or nation, however, has no single decision maker. It is a power structure, and within all power structures one or more individuals decide, often coercively, what the actions of all individuals within the group or nation will be. A group or nation (unless each individual is guilty as an individual) should not, therefore, be considered estranged. There should be no collective guilt.

Although, collectively, groups should not be considered estranged, individual members of the group are a part of the past (and present) that affected the behavior. They should, therefore, assume some responsibility. As individuals, they are not guilty of all the specific acts done by other members of the group if they did not also commit them. They are, however, guilty of having helped create the past (or present) of the group or nation to which they belong, having contributed sins of both commission and omission. They are responsible for this.

Why does God permit sin and estrangement to come into the world providing the means for people to destroy themselves? Is this consistent with what might be expected of a loving God? Tillich suggests that to deny the presence of sin and estrangement, and the evil that results, is to deny people their freedom. God does not give a person freedom and then withdraw it, as freedom is a basic ingredient of a person's nature. Freedom of choice is what makes humans different from all else that lives. Without it, people would be nothing but by puppets of God.

The price of freedom: sinfulness—According to Tillich, all humans exist within a state of sinfulness and to some degree are estranged from God though their essential nature is good (Genesis 1:31). The price one pays for their sinfulness manifests itself in one of a number of ways, through self-destruction, death and its anxiety, suffering, despair and suicide.

Self-destruction is the result of one or more of the three basic sins, unbelief, hubris and concupiscence. As one's sinful ways become increasingly exaggerated, one's life becomes increasingly endangered. One may suffer a total breakdown and lose their hold on the world, literally "falling apart." The world is no longer meaningful. Rather than progressing toward one's full potential (essential goodness), as God would wish, one may develop in all directions without any definite aim in mind. His or her behavior becomes distorted with the goal of simply wishing to be different. The opposite may also occur. When dominated by sin (particularly concupiscence—the drive for knowledge, sex and power), a person's ability to relate positively with others is destroyed. One tries to control the behavior of others, forcing them to conform with one's opinions and ideas. Those who do this become rigid and inflexible. This phenomenon is not limited to an individual, as aimless change or rigidity may occur within an entire society. According to Tillich, the industrial society of the West is a good example of aimless change.

Anxiety about death is the result of being separated from God by sin and estrangement. When separated from God, one becomes fearful and anxious about one's ultimate fate, death. One becomes obsessively frightened at the thought of dying though death is in conformity with biblical religion, which asserts that people are naturally mortal. According to the Old Testament (Genesis 3:19), humans come from dust and return to dust.

According to Tillich, some anxiety about death and non-being is natural and present in all of humanity. Like the beating of the heart, it is always present, although one is not necessarily aware of it. The biblical description of Jesus' death on the cross confirms this natural anxiety of humans. However, as a person becomes increasingly dominated by sin, the anxiety resulting from the fear of death becomes an ever deeper despair.

Suffering may be either meaningful or meaningless, according to Tillich. All suffering results from one of two causes, through natural catastrophes or through sinfulness. Both kinds of suffering can be meaningful, however, if one develops the ability to rise above the suffering. To some extent, this is dependent upon the individual person who is suffering and how he or she responds to the suffering, including its causes.

According to Tillich, meaningless suffering often occurs as a result of what he calls loneliness. When one is lonely, union with other persons is most often a way of trying to overcome it, although it often results in hostilities between people rather than a defeat of loneliness. In order to explain what happens in this process, Tillich distinguishes between the solitude which belongs to people who are in unity with God, and the loneliness of those under the domination of sin. Tillich suggests that all people are essentially alone in the world. The more alone, the more conscious they may become of themselves as individuals in harmony with God. When not under the domination of sin, they develop a centeredness and harmony that provide them the ability to live successfully. This is called solitude by Tillich. A solitude through which one develops a meaningful relationship with God, is a prerequisite to loving relationships with others.

People who are under the domination of sin do not develop a meaningful relationship with God, and can only experience loneliness. Loneliness, in contrast to solitude, is intolerable. It is frightening. It is emptiness. It is disharmony. One is driven by one's lonely life to the "group." In searching for a means to defeat loneliness one surrenders to the group's spirit and culture. One continues to seek out other individuals but is rejected, as they, most often, are also in a state of loneliness and disharmony. Rejection becomes hostility between individuals, resulting in great suffering.

Another form of meaningless suffering, other than loneliness, comes from insecurity, uncertainty, and meaninglessness (nothing has worth). This is true, though some insecurity and uncertainty are an integral part of a person's essential nature, and are necessary to the development of a fulfilling life. Without some insecurity and uncertainty, there is a lack of a stimulus that is needed to realize one's full potential. If, under the domination of sin, insecurity and uncertainty expand beyond a person's need for development, the situation changes. Insecurity leads to despair about the possibility of a fulfilling life, and uncertainty leads toward a refusal to accept any truth, no matter how valid. Everything becomes a negative.

The destructive character of insecurity and uncertainty can be seen in the way people try to escape the destructiveness. They strive to eliminate all insecurity and uncertainty in their lives. Any threat to their security or any challenge to their certainty produces defenses. Some defenses may be brutal, some fanatical, some dishonest, and all non-effective and destructive for there is no security and certainty within life. Those who are threatened by insecurity and uncertainty become restless, empty, and cynical. In a worst case scenario they may use force against those who represent the threat, resulting in death and destruction. In a nation, insecurity and uncertainty may result in war and persecution.

Despair and suicide are called structures of destruction by Tillich. There are many people who have been disenfranchised by our current industrial society. People have been treated as cogs in the process of a mechanizing industry. They have been considered, essentially, no different from the machines themselves. They have been manipulated, overlooked, devalued, driven into loneliness, despair, emptiness and meaninglessness. Tillich takes exception, however, to those who suggest that this is entirely the result of an industrial society. There are many of what Tillich calls "structures of destruction" within society that contribute to this process and have always been present in history.

Despair occurs when one's life consists of endless turmoil and conflict and a person realizes the reality of what "could have been" rather than "what is." A great deal of pain is experienced because there is no perceptible way of filling "the gap." One cannot escape from the situation, because the situation exists within the individual. One cannot run away from oneself. Suicide may appear to be attractive in this situation and may appear as the only means left for escape.

The act of suicide is singled out for special moral and religious condemnation by many religious communities. Life is sacred, and to take one's own life is seen as an unforgivable sin. The act of suicide is perceived as excluding the person from the possibility of God's saving grace. Tillich does not believe that it is a mortal sin as it is not consistent with the very essence of God's love.

Tillich believes that it is hard to argue against suicide not providing a means to escape despair. He, however, does not believe that suicide is a viable option to life, at least for himself, as, within this life, God is working creatively within us. Where there is God there is hope! We are never cut off completely from God, not even in the depths of despair.

The condition of despair is represented theologically in the symbol of the "wrath of God," a much debated symbol within theological circles. For instance, if God is a God of love, as believed by most theologians, how can God also be a God of wrath? This split is seemingly re-enforced by many biblical passages that refer to both a God of love and a God of wrath.

Tillich suggests that if one sees God as a wrathful God, this may very well be a measure of how one sees and understands God, rather than as an accurate representation of the true nature of God. Those who perceive God as wrathful may not have room for a loving God. In Martin Luther's words "as you believe God, so you have God." Wrath, in this view, refers to perception rather than reality.

The Search for Christ: Union with God

People in many parts of the world are searching for a personal relationship with the Christ and union with God. No person on one's own, however, can do this as all people are immersed in a sinful society. As has previously been discussed, people are free to act, but their freedom is limited by the world of sinfulness, past and present. The inability to rise above one's sinfulness is called "the bondage of the will" by Martin Luther, St. Augustine, and the Apostle Paul. "The bondage of the will" is the inability of people to effect a union with God on their own, try as they may to do so. Only God's love (which is a free and unmerited gift from God to all people), can take one out of bondage and into a New Being.

A New Being—In much of the world, religion and culture are largely determined by the expectation of a New Being that transformed a reality in which "a Messiah" has conquered estrangement. This is true in Judaism, Christianity, Islam, Hinduism, and even within the ancient religions of Persia. In each of these instances, the New Being represents a changed reality based on the assumption that humans are basically good despite the degree to which an individual is estranged. In Christianity, the physical reality of a New Being occurred almost two thousand years ago in Jesus the Christ (the Messiah). Although Jesus manifested himself as the New Being then, the full realization of the Kingdom of God, did not arrive with him—it continues its process of arriving through God's continuous revelation today.

According to Tillich, within Judaism the symbol "Messiah" represents a king that is yet to come and within Christianity a king that has already come in the form of Jesus. In both instances, the Messiah is perceived to have many powers attributed to kings of that period. The Messiah, the "anointed one," will conquer the enemy and establish peace and justice. Individuals will then enter a new reality in which the Messiah has conquered sin and estrangement.

Attempts at self-salvation—Trying to overcome one's sinful existence without the love of God, and the reality of a New Being, have been tried through all of religious history and has resulted only in failure and despair. Tillich describes how these attempts have been made. He places them into five categories: (1) theological, (2) legalistic, (3) ascetic, (4) mystical, and (5) sacramental, doctrinal, and emotional.

Theologism, an exclusively theological viewpoint relies on an intellectual approach to Christ and union with God without a New Being taking place in the person. Unfortunately, this is simply an attempt at self-salvation and is doomed to failure.

Legalism is one of the more usual ways of attempting self-salvation. The law, as found in the scriptures, describes the essential nature of people when totally within the realm of God. When individual persons, however, knowledgeable of the law, however, see the difference between "the way they really are" and the "ought-to-be" of the law, they become full of anxiety and guilt as it is impossible to attain what ought-to-be totally on one's own. Disregarding "the bondage of the will," believing that one has the personal power to develop one's total potential, can only result in failure. Only God's love is able to produce a New Being in one's life.

Asceticism is another means of attempting self-salvation. It eliminates from one's life as many objects of desire as possible. In the extreme, this is a monastic system. According to Tillich, asceticism fails because it tries to force union with God by conscious acts of self-denial. The roots of sin in human nature do not disappear, however, as they are simply present in a repressed form. They often reappear as exaggerated fantasy and strange behavior through acts that inflict pain on oneself and others as in fanatical religious cults.

Mysticism refers to the divine as present in one's personal experience. In this sense, mysticism is an important part of all religions. A religion without a "God present" is nothing more than a system of non-religious laws, regulations, or codes.

In this context, mysticism has nothing to do with self-salvation. Attempts at mystical self- salvation occur when one tries to effect a union with God through "mental exercises." The attempt, in most forms of Eastern and Western mysticism, is to try to transcend all of life's realities in order to unite with God.

As far as Tillich is concerned, this leads to failure. A real union with God is never reached by the mystic as the types of ecstasy usually associated with attempts at union are most often followed by long periods of depression and sometimes despair. A person's estranged life remains the same. One's "real life" existence is not "dealt" with through these kinds of experiences as the conditions of existence remain unchanged.

Sacramental, doctrinal, or emotional acts, according to Tillich, do not provide salvation in and of themselves. Only grace (love), through the power of one's New Being in Christ can conquer one's estranged condition and provide salvation. The sacraments are a very important part of Tillich's theology, however, serving as acts of union with God.

Tillich suggests that too often the act of participating in a sacrament is distorted by the need to "do it right." Too much emphasis is put on the "appropriate" way to observe a particular sacrament rather than concentrating on how the act provides a union between God and the individual.

Regarding doctrine, some religious groups emphasize "the pure doctrine" of "obedience to the word of God" as the means of salvation. Obedience is demanded to the letter of the law contained in the Bible even though its meaning is not always obvious and it may be contradictory. Doctrinal obedience then becomes obedience to a person or group of person's particular interpretation of the Bible. This leads to a blind acceptance of a biblical interpretation or a church doctrine with no critical questioning possible.

The doctrine "justification by faith," as an example, has been distorted by blind acceptance. Faith, as far as many churches are concerned, is simply a matter of orally declaring one's belief in God after which God accepts you the sinner. According to Tillich, faith perceived in this manner is nothing more than an intellectual affirmation. Questions of whether one truly believes or whether one believes because one wants to, or whether belief is actually necessary for salvation, leads to great anxiety and an inner struggle between trying to be honest and desiring to be saved.

Emotionalism, as in pietism, requires a personal commitment through a conversion experience, followed by the devotional dedication of one's life to God. This is one way of finding union with God. However, when distorted by a "triggered" desire for emotions, which are most often artificially created by a revivalisticly charged experience, piety becomes a "tool" that one uses to transform oneself. When this occurs, anxiety and fanaticism are the result and it too fails to produce a lasting union with God.

The basis for all true religion, according to Tillich, involves a personal relationship with God that places God above all other considerations in one's life.

Commentary

Although many theologians agree with Tillich's premise that humans are essentially good, essential goodness appears to be contradicted by the presence of so much evil in the world. How can humans be essentially good and yet involve themselves in numerous and repetitive acts of inhumanity, such as the ethnic cleansing in what used to be Yugoslavia, the holocaust of World War II, and the strategic bombing by Allied air forces during this same war?

Abraham Maslow, often called the father of humanistic psychology, addresses the matter of humanity's inherent goodness through his research on human behavior. He concludes that the natural progression of humans is upward in a hierarchy that concludes with their entry into a process of "self-actualization," that is similar to a state of "goodness." This hierarchy was discovered through clinical observation (involving hundreds of individuals) and is as follows: [5]

[5.] Abraham Maslow, *Motivation and Personality* (New York: Harper and Brothers, 1954), pp. 35-58, 149-180.

the need for self-actualization (development), to become everything one
can become.
a sense of esteem,
a sense of belonging and love,
safety needs, and
satisfaction of physiological needs such as hunger and thirst.

Maslow found that those who developed the furthest up the ladder often enjoyed a significantly better relationship of trust and influence among their peers well beyond considerations of their respective wealth or position. He also found that most people progressed along this hierarchy though some simply did not fit the pattern.

A second theological premise of Tillich's is that God's aim for humans is the development of their potential—their essential goodness—within the framework of God's love. The question has been raised: "Can we truly appreciate the good, the fullness of life in Cod's creation, if we haven't experienced, first hand, what the underside of life is like? Can one appreciate the good if there has been no experience of the bad? Is some degree of insecurity and uncertainty, stress and anxiety, confronting the possibility of failure, necessary for one's highest development?" According to Tillich, confronting adversity is not absolutely necessary, though he agrees that it is an important ingredient in the development of many people's lives.

Rollo May, a leader in humanistic psychology re-enforces Tillich's premise when he suggests that:

> *...anxiety (insecurity and uncertainty) helps us to get across a*
> *busy street. Without anxiety we would be ground to mincemeat*
> *within ten minutes. If we had more anxiety at Hitler's ascension,*
> *we would have been better able to act against it.*[6]

[6.] Janet Silver Grant, "Doing's more important than feeling, says psychologist," *The Tribune*, Oakland, CA (May 16,1990), Sec. D, p.1.

In his work with industry, Frederick Herzberg found that some insecurity was essential to the development of employees as they advanced into increasingly responsible positions. The ability to succeed or fail, particularly in their first major job out of school, had a direct correlation with long-range organizational success. Organizational success has a closer correlation with the nature of the first job than the particular university that one attended, grade point average maintained, or origin of birth.

Discussion

1. Discuss Tillich's image of God as "the source of all being" and compare it with images that you may have. Does God orchestrate all the events that take place in the world and to you personally, some of them, or all of them? Include within your discussion the question of "Why God permits evil?"

2. If God influences outcomes only, what is the role or value of petitionary prayer? .

3. Do you agree that all sins are derived from one, or a combination, of Tillich's three basic sins? What are the basic sins involved in racism, sexism and hate? How do they relate to each other?

4. Are all people basically good and learn to be bad?

5. Should we be held completely responsible for what we do, given Tillich's explanation concerning the influences that bear on freedom of action? How should this be taken into account in the courts?

6. What does Tillich mean by the "structures of destruction?" Develop a list. Are they inevitable?

7. Do you agree that stress and suffering are critical to one's development? Should a person consciously invite suffering for the sake of personal development?

8. What does Tillich mean by a New Being?

9. Are you satisfied with the descriptions of self-salvation? Does the issue of self-salvation help you to look at your own life? Does Tillich's discussion of the perils of self-salvation lead to one's being able to do most anything that he wants if he "truly" believes in Jesus the Christ?

CHAPTER 2

Finding The Christ: What Then?

Chapter Introduction

Tillich exams a wide range of issues regarding the nature of Jesus the Christ and the manner in which the church represents this nature to the world. Of great importance is the paradox of Jesus' being fully human and also fully divine. How can this be? Tillich acknowledges that he does not fully understand this mystery. He suggests, however, to believe otherwise is to discount Jesus' divine ministry to the world as well as his humanity seen in the pain he experienced as a human and his death on the cross.

Who is the Christ?

Christianity is based on the belief that Jesus entered the world as a human being, shared the reality of the human experience and, as the Christ, prevailed over it, as estranged and as sinful as the world might be. He is both human and divine.

The name Jesus Christ is a combination of the two aspects of Jesus. The name Jesus refers to a man who was raised in Nazareth two thousand years ago, and the word "Christ" recognizes that he received a special role to establish the reign of God in Israel and in the entire world. He is the Christos (Greek)—the "anointed one"—the Messiah—the expected deliverer of the Jews. Therefore, the name Jesus Christ is better expressed as "Jesus the Christ."

The New Testament takes very seriously the lineage of Jesus beginning with Abraham and extending through the line of King David. This is the community from which Jesus comes and from which the New Being arises. In selecting the apostles, Jesus symbolically connects the twelve tribes of Israel (the past) with the twelve apostles who start the church (the future). In this manner, the New Testament shows that the New Being, present in Jesus the Christ, has been present throughout all of history.

According to Tillich, proving the existence of a "historical Jesus," through a search of documents other than the Bible, provides a minimum of reliable facts about the man Jesus of Nazareth and his life. This could lead one to conclude that Jesus did not exist. This is not so, however, as it only indicates that it is not provable through historical inquiry. The historical method of examination used by biblical scholars, however, simply asks how trustworthy the records are. It does this, not as a matter of faith, but based upon a close examination of the biblical account, and other documents independent of the Bible, including those that might have influenced or inspired the biblical account. The more exhaustive the examination, the more there appears to be little evidence in support of a "historical Jesus" separate from the biblical account.

According to Tillich, the struggles that Protestantism has undergone in its efforts to prove that Jesus actually existed has led to no conclusive results. The effort has not been wasted, however, as it has resulted in providing new ways of looking at the biblical text. Through the process of historical inquiry the biblical text has been categorized into: (1) that which is historically probable, based on the presence of empirical evidence, (2) that which is legendary (a story handed down for generations and popularly believed to have a historical basis, although not verifiable), and (3) myth (a traditional story of unknown authorship, ostensibly with a historical basis, usually involving the exploits of gods and heroes).

Categorization has important consequences to the systematic theologian, according to Tillich. The three categories provide a multifaceted way of studying and interpreting the Bible. They avoid the fundamentalist's literalism that tries to make all scripture literally true no matter how contradictory or mythological.

Using the best scholarship available, historical analysis makes a very positive contribution to theology by finding the sources of individual passages and their meaning. Though this type of analysis provides a positive and fruitful means of biblical review, it does so with some risk, as its approach opens the possibility of making all biblical literature suspect in its authority. Historical research could come to the conclusion that there simply was no "historical" Jesus of Nazareth. Some scholars have come to this conclusion, although most have not.

Some fundamentalist theologians attempt to overcome the results of historical analysis through the power of faith, suggesting that faith can cancel the results. According to Tillich, however, faith alone cannot make a legend or myth found in the Bible historically verifiable, nor can it make that which is improbable (based upon historical inquiry) highly probable. Faith cannot make something that is not historically verifiable, historically verifiable. Tillich goes on to suggest:

> ...concrete biblical material is not guaranteed by faith in respect to empirical factuality; but it is guaranteed as an adequate expression of the transforming power of the New Being in Jesus the Christ....[7]

---

7. Tillich, II, p.115.

Faith can verify that there is a reality, a "something," that has created the faith, but it cannot attest to matters of historical inquiry. In the same sense, historical inquiry can only verify the results of historical inquiry. Nothing more.

In every respect the New Testament is the basic source document for the picture of Jesus as the Christ. So-called "liberal" theologians tried to go behind these source documents to get a clearer picture of Jesus of Nazareth through historical analysis. This has been a failure.[8] The first three Gospels (commonly called the Synoptic Gospels, as they give parallel summaries of the life and teachings of Jesus), are the most important source documents to theologians. Tillich reminds us though, that the Christian faith cannot be built solely on this limited view; that the fourth Gospel, John, and the remainder of the New Testament are equally important. The first three Gospels give the basis upon which Jesus is understood as the Christ, while the remainder of the New Testament elaborates on this picture.

Jesus the Christ: The New Being

The apostles originally expected that the second coming of Christ would occur immediately following his earthly ministry, and certainly during their lifetimes. With the second coming, a new eon would begin in which evil would be abolished. This expectation was not fulfilled and the nature of the world and its estrangement from God continued. This became a major issue in the early days of the church and among Jesus' apostles. The expectation either had to be changed, or the very foundation of the new church would be shattered.

---

8. Since Tillich's day, and extending to today, a group of scholars calling themselves "The Jesus Seminar" have done considerable research on the historical Jesus. Their work has concentrated on an examination of the Synoptic Gospels and a determination of what part of the Synoptics was actually the words of Jesus.

The apostles, through the resurrection (Easter), and a life transforming experience when the divine Spirit descended upon them (Pentecost), gained a new understanding of what the "new eon" meant. Rather than an immediate second coming of Christ and the abolishment of sin, the "new eon" would appear in the lives of individual persons as a New Being, transforming one's life in a manner similar to the apostles' transformation at Pentecost. The hope of humanity for a "new eon" has been fully realized in Jesus as the Christ, who is the ultimate ideal.

Tillich also speaks of the power of the New Being in another sense. The New Being removes an individual from under a law of judgment to an existence in which the law becomes the very essence of the person. The law is internalized within the person and no longer exists as a separate "you shall" or as a law of judgment. A person is, instead, motivated to do that which is "intrinsically right," rather than motivated from a fear of judgment and punishment.

The New Being in Jesus as the Christ: the victory over estrangement—To try to separate the various aspects of the life and works of Jesus the Christ is to do him a disservice. Jesus' character is inadequately understood if one transposes the *teachings* of Jesus into doctrinal statements about who Jesus is, who God is, and how humans must behave in relation to doctrinal and ethical laws. If this occurs, Jesus as the Christ, is replaced by the great moral teacher Jesus of Nazareth.

If one emphasizes the *deeds* of Jesus and the need for them to be imitated, the same situation results. Activity in resolving the problems of society can certainly be admired, but over emphasis can make us imitators of Christ, according to Tillich. We are in danger of following social, ritualistic or ascetic prescriptions, rather than becoming a New Being in the totality of Christ.

Finally, regarding the *suffering* Jesus, it is true that only through his suffering and death could he have participated directly in the suffering and estrangement experienced by humanity. This, and the resurrection, symbolizes his victory over the world's estranged and sinful condition. This is important but again it must not dominate our understanding of the totality of the Christ.

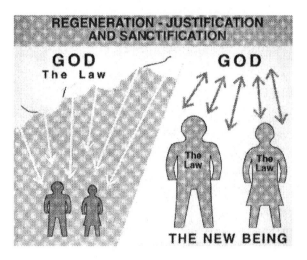

Jesus the Christ must not be reduced to individual parts, with each able to "stand on its own." The singular point that Tillich makes is that all parts of Jesus must be taken together if one wishes to see the totality of Christ as the New Being in the lives of others. To simply see him as a maker of the "law," or as the great "ethical teacher" is to do him a gross injustice.

Jesus the Christ, was victorious as a human over the world's estrangement, although he experienced great anxiety in regard to his death on the cross. Jesus not only experienced the full anxiety of death, but from the time of his birth, experienced want, mental anxiety, loneliness and rejection. He lived and experienced life as others live and experience it; at the same time, he was deeply affected by the misery in which he saw humanity existing and by those who turned to him for help. His was a life of tension.

Jesus existed in this world with the same limits placed upon him as those placed on other human beings. As everyone else, he was subject to error. This is evident in his conception of the universe, his judgments about people, his interpretation of history, and his perceptions of the end of the world. Jesus was hesitant about accepting the messianic role (Luke 7:19-22), and had doubts about his own relationship with God, and was in despair about dying on the cross. (Mt. 27:46) Doubts and anxieties were essential to the human side of Jesus' nature.

Throughout history, existence in the world has been full of uncertainty caused by the difficulties involved in relationships with individuals, with groups, or with various other scenarios that have confronted people daily. One of the major ambiguities that confronted Jesus the Christ was the relationship between his greatness and his life within a world of sin and estrangement. Jesus participated in a world such as this.

The nature and function of Christian dogma and its symbols— Dogma is the statement of "truth" within which a person or community lives. The development of dogma was very important to the early church Fathers as it was meant to preserve the Christian message against misrepresentation from outside as well as from inside the church.

Tillich asks two questions concerning dogma: (1) Did it keep the Christian message intact? and (2) did the symbols used in the dogma adequately express what the Christian church wanted to say? He suggests that the answer to the first question is yes, the dogma did keep the Christian message intact. The answer to the second question, however, is no, the symbols did not express the Christian message as well as desired.

In the latter regard, the inadequacies of the symbols used in the dogma were due to two things: (1) they were not able to fully express the depth and breadth of the message of the New Being in Jesus as the

Christ, as this is the deepest, most profound, most meaningful message possible, and (2) the symbols used in the writing of the New Testament, two thousand years ago, came almost exclusively from within the realm of Greek philosophy. Symbols derived from the Greek era, were limited and were dependent on such mythically divine figures as Apollo and Dionysus.

The Christian message was Hellenized (Greek in character), as this was the prevailing culture of the time. Hellenized symbols and ideas included the Greek word Christ, translated from the Hebrew word Messiah (the one chosen by God). This was when the title Christ began to be used as a part of Jesus' proper name, Jesus Christ, rather than Jesus the chosen one of God. This resulted in much of the original meaning being lost. Another result of Hellenization was the emphasis in the Christian message on redeeming the world to a higher level, heaven, with little emphasis on the transformation of life within the world as it exists. The balance between these two views continues to be controversial within the church today.

Tillich concludes that we should not assign blame for problems within Christianity to the inadequacy of the symbols and concepts found in church dogma. Instead, we must pursue with vigor the real substance of the Christian Gospel (the Good News), not letting the full meaning of the dogma be limited by an inadequacy of expression centuries old. Theology must constantly search for better ways to reveal the Gospel message.

A major problem in the study of Christ is how to best explain the relation between Jesus, the human, and Jesus, the divine. Any lessening of Jesus' human nature takes away his truly human experience within the world's estranged existence; any decrease of his divine nature results in a lessening of his power to influence a sinful world.

He is indeed, fully human and fully divine, which Tillich admits is something of a puzzle. Symbols and concepts have been inadequate in explaining these two natures, resulting in many struggles within the church. Many leading theologians have emphasized the divinity of Jesus; others have emphasized his human nature. In spite of this struggle over dogma, the early church at Nicaea, in 325 A.D. and Chalcedon in 451 A.D., continued to preserve both the divine and human concept of Jesus the Christ. According to Tillich, new symbols and concepts must be found that capture the full humanness and divinity of the Christ as described in the Gospels.

Tillich tells us that there are many other aspects of the life of Jesus in the New Testament that serve as important symbols to our Christian faith. The "death of Jesus on the cross" and the "resurrection," are perhaps the two most important.

The death of Jesus on the cross is the occurrence from which the remainder of the New Testament receives its meaning. Jesus the Christ, entered the world, making himself vulnerable to the whole range of depravities within which the world exists, yet never yielding to the sinfulness of humanity. Jesus' death on the cross, as a symbol, or as an occurrence, represents how Jesus defeated all temptations, including rejection of his kinship with God while on the cross.

The symbol "resurrection of the Christ" is of equal importance, as it symbolizes how the New Being in the Christ is victorious over sin and death. Jesus was raised from the dead and joined his father in heaven. One of the earlier symbols that parallels the resurrection, is the story of the transfiguration of Jesus: "….And he was transfigured before them: and his face did shine as the sun, and his raiment was as white as the light…" (Mt. 17:2)

Other symbols of importance include the stories of Jesus' humble birth, his flight to Egypt, the early threat to his life by the political forces in power, his betrayal by Judas, his manner of burial. These must all be understood symbolically as ways that Jesus joined us in our estranged society.

The debate concerning whether the events of Jesus life are literally true as described in the New Testament has masked the importance of the events as symbols representing God's truth. Tillich takes particular issue with the miracle stories found in the Bible. He believes the emphasis on their literal truth as "proof" of Jesus' divine power misses the point. He sees these stories as only symbolic, attesting to how the New Being in Christ can overcome the self-destructive forces that plague the world. As far as Tillich is concerned, whether they are, in and of themselves, literally true, is doubtful. God's presence and power should not be perceived as interfering with natural processes in a unilateral, magical way. It is the power of God's natural laws and the power of the New Being, together, working within the human spirit, that overcomes the self-destructive consequences of the world's sinfulness.

Symbols must not be ignored or discarded because of doubts concerning whether the events described actually occurred. Their meaning needs to be interpreted and re-interpreted within the church, in preaching and teaching, and in personal devotion.

Salvation

The word salvation comes from the Greek "salvus" whose original meaning was "to heal." Tillich believes this meaning of salvation is much more appropriate than the commonly understood version of "being saved for eternal life."

According to Tillich, it is impossible to separate the idea of salvation from healing, which, theologically, means the reuniting of humans with God, with themselves, and with the entire world. Salvation as healing is the very essence of Jesus' ministry to the world. Although the organized church has not always acted as the world's greatest healer, Christ's presence has produced an ever evolving humanity, containing a broad array of positively oriented religions and cultures. Imperfect as they may be, the churches, together, have kept humans from blowing up the world. This is so in spite of the world's bent to destroy itself.

Unfortunately, according to Tillich, much of the historical view of salvation emphasizes a belief that salvation is "being saved for eternal life," either total or not at all. In this view, total salvation is dependent upon one's acceptance of the saving power of Jesus the Christ. Total salvation is equivalent to being taken into an everlasting state of blessedness; the lack of salvation results in a state of everlasting pain or eternal death. If this concept is taken literally, suggests Tillich, most people, past, present, and future will be condemned to everlasting pain or eternal death, if for no other reason than having never heard of Jesus.

Tillich believes, instead, that salvation must be understood as a healing and saving power through the New Being in all of history and, as such, must be seen in a different light. No human is totally healed, or saved, even though experiencing a personal relationship with Jesus the Christ. All humans need the healing power of the New Being.

Atonement—Christ is the Savior, the Mediator, and the Redeemer of humanity through the power of his love. This love, according to Tillich, no matter under what name it is known, has been, and will be available to humanity through all of history.

When a person is encompassed by the New Being in Jesus the Christ, a process called "atonement" begins. Atonement is that process that allows a person to overcome the past, starting a new life in Jesus the Christ. There are two parts to this process: (1) the appearance of the New Being in one's life, and (2) that which happens to a person as a result. Without both parts, atonement does not take place. According to Tillich, there are some important principles and occurrences regarding atonement that must be clearly understood:

1. The atoning process is created by God and God alone. An individual may elect to participate in it.

2. There is no conflict between God's love and God's justice. Justice is the action form of love. Without it, love would be sheer sentimentality.

3. A person's guilt and fear of punishment is removed through the atoning process. This does not overlook the reality of one's continued sinfulness, however.

4. In the cross of the Christ, God assumes the consequences of the world's sin. This is done through the death and suffering of the innocent son of God, Jesus the Christ.

5. With the presence of the New Being in one's life, one becomes a part of Christ's suffering on the cross. This empowers one to overcome the estrangement of the world.

Commentary

There is a continuing debate within the churches concerning whether the Bible is literally true and without error. Some fundamentalist theologians try to "prove" the accuracy of the Bible through the power of their faith in spite of the many questions raised by historical analysis concerning its accuracy and the inconsistencies of interpretation and obvious conflicts in the text of the Bible. To illustrate this latter point, a minister friend included in his Sunday morning sermon, a story from the Christian Century Magazine as follows:

> *The people who operate Looper Motor Sales—"Your Christian Car Lot"—in Hickory, North Carolina, apparently disapprove of having Geraldine Ferraro or any woman run for the office of vice-president...Their advertisement...urges the reader...to "Vote Republican." The reasons given consist entirely of Bible verses, two of which are 1 Peter 3:7, which says that the wife is the "weaker vessel," and 1 Corinthians 11:3, which says that "the head of the woman is the man."*

A few days after reading the article my minister friend happened to run across a bumper sticker on a car he was following that read: "God said it. I believe it. That settles it."

These may be exaggerated illustrations of problems in biblical interpretation but they do serve to illustrate the point, "what is the correct interpretation?" Here is some more:

> we find that people can and often do quote the Bible on opposite sides of the same issue. My gun-owning friend quotes Jesus as saying, "go buy a sword." What happens if I tell him that Jesus also said "all who take the sword will perish by the sword?" (Mt. 26:52)....The Bible says, "You shall not kill"...yet the death penalty was instituted by God following the flood (Gen. 9) and Christ ratified it when he said that he had come not to abolish the law but fulfill it.... The "right-to-life" group quotes' the Bible against abortion (Ex. 21:22-23); the "free choice" people note that God approves it under some circumstances (Hosea 13:16).... Before the Civil War the southern slave owners liked to refer to the example of Paul who sent a runaway slave back to his owner (Philemon), and who told slaves to be "obedient" to their masters (Eph. 6:15). But the northern abolitionists and promoters of the "underground railway" had a text of their own: "you shall not give up to a master a slave who has escaped...he shall dwell with you...you shall not oppress him" (DT. 23:15-16). [9]

Though Tillich takes issue with those who believe in the literal accuracy of the Bible, he does not believe that the issue is of great theological significance. He suggests that the Christian church would be better

---

[9.] *The Interpreter's Dictionary of the Bible* (Nashville, Abingdon Press 1962), Vol. I, p. 727.

served if its attention was focused on the Bible as a "symbolic" expression of the transforming power of the New Being in Jesus the Christ, rather than whether it is literally true. Whether literally true or not, the truly important point is the theological truth that is symbolically represented. This is not dependent upon its literal accuracy.

Discussion

1. What if the importance of Jesus' being seen as divine and at the same time human?

2. What is the relationship between the findings of historical inquiry, and faith, as Tillich discusses it. Is the "fact" of Jesus life on this earth a necessary basis for your faith?

3. Is the Bible the authoritative word of God and, as such, inerrant? Why does Tillich believe that the debate regarding in errancy masks the importance of many biblical events?

4. What does Tillich mean when he talks about "the law" becoming one's very essence? What might be the practical ramifications of this?

5. Describe and discuss what Tillich means by the power of the New Being. How is this different, or is it, than being "born again?"

6. Discuss the relationship between salvation and atonement?

CHAPTER 3

The Uncertainties Of Life: The Search For Security

Chapter Introduction

It is important to Tillich that his theology encompass the human condition. Much of this chapter describes the human condition by first suggesting a system of classification within which human beings can be seen in relationship to all other living things. Then, with human beings placed at the top of the evolutionary ladder, he describes the natural processes of human growth, sharing at the same time, the inherent ambiguities involved. Tillich's purpose is not to present an exhaustive treatise on the problems of human existence, it is, rather, to provide one an overview of life as it is lived, and then, from this perspective, address the problems of human existence from a theological perspective. The realities of existence serve as the foundation to Tillichian theology.

In recovering the elements of human nature that were suppressed by the psychology of consciousness, existentialism and contemporary theology should become allies and analyze the character of existence in all of its manifestations, the unconscious as well as the conscious. The systematic theologian cannot do this alone; he needs the help of creative representatives of existentialism in all realms of culture. He needs the support of the practical explorers of the human predicament, such as ministers, educators, psychoanalysts, and counselors. The theologian must reinterpret the traditional religious symbols and theological concepts in the light of the material he receives from these people. He must be aware of the fact that terms like "sin" and "judgment" have lost not their truth but rather an expressive power that can be regained only if they are filled with the insights into human nature that existentialism (including depth psychology) has given to us.[10]

Unity of Life

Dimensions and realms—To illustrate the natural unity of life, Tillich classifies all that exists in God's creation into *dimensions and realms*. There is so much diversity within the world that some system of examination is necessary. The concept of dimensions and realms suggests a hierarchial pyramid, which is not to Tillich's liking, but he uses it as it provides the ability to examine life from a three dimensional standpoint: depth, breadth and height.

The *designation of a dimension* can best be understood as a combination of dimensions with no single dimension predominating. Examples of dimensions used by Tillich are the inorganic, the organic, the spirit, the psychological and the historical.

The concept of realm describes a section of life in which one dimension predominates over the others that are present within the realm. It may include within itself the inorganic and the organic dimensions as well as others. The key difference is that one dimension predominates over the others. The human realm, as an example, made up of many dimensions, is generally thought of as being predominated by the psychological dimension. The organic realm is made up of both the organic and inorganic dimensions with the organic predominating.

---

[10]. Paul Tillich, *Systematic Theology* (Chicago: University of Chicago Press, 1957), II, pp. 27-28.

The *concept of dimensions* is used to illustrate a basic premise of Tillich's theology: God's purpose in creating living things is to have them maximize their total potential. In a human being it is the realization of the highest possible attainment in psychological and spiritual development. For other living things it is the highest possible attainment consistent with their particular life form. He illustrates this premise by pointing out that a tree seedling will grow into a tree as tall and healthy as its genetic factors will allow it. This is God's purpose. In the same sense, human beings are meant to grow and develop to their ultimate possibilities.

Tillich classifies everything that exists into:

1. the spiritual dimension,

2. the psychological dimension,

3. the organic dimension, and

4. the inorganic dimension.

Within this framework, some dimensions are dependent upon the development of others. For example, the organic dimension is dependent upon the inorganic; the psychological dimension is dependent upon the organic; and the spiritual dimension is dependent upon the psychological. This hierarchial pyramid suggests that there are differences in value between dimensions, and to some degree this is true, according to Tillich.

All dimensions owe their existence to the presence of the inorganic dimension which is placed at the bottom of the pyramid. With the exception of the inorganic, each dimension is dependent to some degree on all those dimensions below it. Tillich suggests that humans are the highest order (although he understands that this is an arguable position), as only within a human does one find all dimensions represented, including that of the spiritual.

In the case of the organic dimension, it evolved out of that of the inorganic. No one knows when this occurred. Obviously the organic dimension exists at a higher and more complex level than the inorganic, if for no other reason than life began within the organic. The psychological dimension evolved out of the organic dimension when the "right" conditions were present in the organic dimension. And the dimension of the spirit evolved from that of the psychological.

The dimension of the spirit appears exclusively within humans and, so far, it is the highest dimension in God's creation. It is important that we gain a greater awareness of its meaning. According to Tillich, the concept of spirit evolved from that of breath (breath and spirit are interchangeable in Semitic languages), with the spirit assuming a separate entity from the body. Later, spirit became mind, with emphasis on the intellect. Today, the spirit is generally reserved for an aspect of the divine, such as the Holy Spirit or divine Spirit, rather than as a part of a human being. As the meaning of spirit disappeared in relationship to humans, it began to disappear in relationship to the divine as well; even within the church. This is so, in part, because without knowing what spirit means in human terms, how can we know what it means in divine terms? A new understanding of the term spirit as a dimension of life is needed, according to Tillich.

Exactly when the spirit evolved from the psychological dimension cannot be determined, although Tillich believes it is reasonable to presume that a long period of struggle was involved. The conditions had to be just right for a leap into a new and dominant dimension. We do know that language had to be a part of when the spiritual dimension came about, as language is essential to the process of thought, and thought to the dimension of the spirit. There is a continuous struggle within humanity between those with great language ability and those without. This, according to Tillich, is an important reason behind the problems of human morality. If one does not have the language necessary to understand—moral action based on understanding is impossible.

Ways within which the Spirit Rises to Dominance over the Psychological Dimension.

The human spirit has a special ability to project thoughts forward and to make independent decisions, although this independence is conditioned somewhat by experiences. According to Tillich, there are three distinct ways that this occurs; from within a person's very essence, illustrating how the spiritual dimension is dominant:

1. the practical way,

2. the theoretical way, and

3. those ways originating from within a person's very essence.

1. *In the practical way*, decisions are based upon the most practical way to address the circumstances needing decision. The difficulty with decisions made in this manner is the lack of consistent decisions and actions. This is particularly true when applied to ethical or political situations. Consistency in these areas requires the development of some criteria based on more than that which is simply practical. As an illustration, suppose a nation's relationship to another nation was based entirely on the practical application of economic self-interest. This would result in many inconsistent policies and decisions as applied to the hundred or more nations in the world. Cooperation between world powers, and world powers with weaker nations, would be most difficult to effect and the whole world would suffer as a result.

2. *The theoretical process* recognizes the difficulties involved in decisions based exclusively on practical considerations. It also recognizes that the opposite extreme, decisions based upon precise laws or rules, also have many difficulties in application. The theoretical approach uses neither of these extremes. It establishes a "hierarchy of values" that serves as a criterion in the decision-making process designed to

secure the highest possible value as a result of the decision. The difficulty with this approach is the determination of the values and their arrangement hierarchically. Who is to say what life's highest values are, particularly those values that control life itself? What makes them valid?

3. *The last process originates from within the very essence of the individual.* Within the dimension of the spirit all thought, decisions, and actions are designed to produce the best possible results accruing from the decisions made. This process includes the practical, without which decisions would lack relevancy, the theoretical, as a hierarchal source of values that projects beyond the simply practical, and a "heaven of values" based on the highest potential achievable.

The question then arises: How is the "heaven of values" decided? What is the highest potential of humanity and the world? According to Tillich, we cannot know exactly what this is, "except that it is good." (Genesis 1:31) The entire sphere of humanity's potential is only partly visible at present. There is no certain way to know how the spirit will affect actions. Making these decisions is a struggle, an adventure and a risk. The struggle toward full potential requires great courage and determination. It involves the possibility of failure. This is one of the most dynamic and exciting aspects of life.

REALIZING ONE'S POTENTIAL THROUGH SELF-INTEGRATION, SELF-CREATIVITY, AND SELF-TRANSCENDENCE

Tillich suggests that there are three processes involved in the realization of one's potential: (1) self-integration, (2) self-creativity, and (3) self-transcendence.

The Self-integration of Life: Problems

The basic step, self-integration, is the process of gaining new experiences, integrating them with all past experiences, resulting in a changed person. During the normal self-integration process, change is generally slow and individuals stay in balance during this process.

Self-integration within the psychological dimension—The process of self-integration is a necessary part of life. It continuously involves growth producing, as well as disintegrating experiences, usually mixed together at any given moment. Regarding disintegration, one's health may be disrupted by the inability to assimilate all the new experiences. As a result, the psychological self disintegrates or suffers from imbalance. The opposite is also possible; rather than too many experiences, the psychological self is afraid of losing itself, becoming indifferent to, or avoiding all outward experiences. This results in indifference and stupor.

The highest form of life in Tillich's hierarchy is the human being. He recognizes that many naturalists do not agree with a distinction that presumes this exalted role for humans, however, he believes it important to consider humans as the highest form of life if for no other reason than to better understand their unique capabilities. When considering humans as the highest form of life one should not confuse the term highest with the most perfect. Perfection refers to the degree to which one reaches one's total potential—easier to reach, perhaps, in lower, less complex forms of life than within humans. The highest, on the other hand, refers to the total number of experiences that can be integrated into a single life. In Tillich's view, this is the human being.

According to Tillich, humans have two distinct and special qualities as the highest form of life: (1) they have the potential to learn from others and their experiences, and (2) they have a capacity for self-awareness, which provides an ability to improve themselves through analyzing their past, present and future behavior. Without self-awareness there is only the immediate experience of reality as it occurs— there is no past remembrance or future anticipation of events and their effect on the individual. It is these two, essentially unique characteristics, that usher in the psychological dimension and the processes of growth through self-integration, self-creativity and self- transcendence

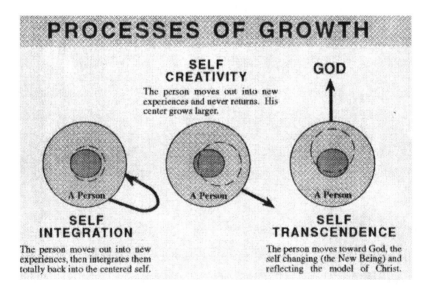

PROCESSES OF GROWTH

SELF CREATIVITY
The person moves out into new experiences and never returns. His center grows larger.

GOD

SELF INTEGRATION
The person moves out into new experiences, then intergrates them totally back into the centered self.

SELF TRANSCENDENCE
The person moves toward God, the self changing (the New Being) and reflecting the model of Christ.

Self-integration within the spiritual dimension—The process of self-integration within the spiritual dimension involves morality.

According to Tillich, a moral act is that which comes naturally from within one's inherently good true being, though it may be perverted by the sinful condition within which one exists. A moral act comes from within not from without such as a law, divine or human.

Tillich makes two presumptions regarding a moral act and morality: (1) human beings, under the dimension of the spirit, are able to project thoughts and decisions forward without being unduly influenced by one's past environment, and, (2) humans are capable of asking questions and getting answers to their questions, as well as following, or not following, someone else's orders or commands.

These presumptions are functions of the spirit and are uniquely possessed by humans. They provide humans the ability to modify their behavior from that conditioned by their experience, to one of loving one's neighbor. According to Tillich, humans have the freedom to " join together in love with all people in spite of physical and cultural differences," (as in the parable of the Good Samaritan—Luke 10:29-37), or humans can choose not to respond. If one responds affirmatively, and in freedom, it is a moral act. If one does not respond, immorality and disintegration are the result.

There are many complexities involved in self-integration. Every person has great potentiality though only some potentialities will be realized and others will not as it depends, in part, on the opportunities or lack of opportunities, which occur within a person's life. Some potentialities will never become real, due to factors beyond the person's control, such as being born poor which limit one's development opportunities in comparison to being born wealthy.

Development opportunities may also be limited due to one's undernourishment or because of the lack of educational opportunity. Sometimes its the matter of quitting school, or going to work so one may eat. This may require giving up those development opportunities available at the time.

Conflicting needs and priorities also restrict a person's ability to reach one's full potential. Often times, one makes a decision regarding the direction of one's life based upon immediate needs, rather than one's future potential. Many people with high potential for college studies fail to go to college because of the immediate financial sacrifices that are involved.

The Self-creativity of Life: Problems

Self-creativity is the second process in realizing one's potential, though it is something of an accelerated version of self-integration. Self-creativity is dominated by a drive to become "other than I am." The person in this process is involved in a substantial change from the old self, rather than in a simple reunion into the former self.

Self-creativity within the dimension of the organic—The concept of self-creativity (also destruction) is best seen within the dimension of the organic. In all processes of growth within the organic, there are the possibilities of both life and death. Progress through life culminates in death. Death is going to happen, either naturally, through a long life, or through a sudden externally imposed occurrence (e.g., as in war). At the moment life begins, we not only begin to live but also begin to die. That which gives us the power of life also provides for its extinction. According to Tillich, the conscious knowledge of this has a significant effect on all human beings.

Growth and destruction are not limited to the internal growth or destruction of an individual being; growth and destruction are also found within the struggle between individual beings. Heraclitus, the 5th Century B.C. Greek Philosopher, addressed this issue by calling war the father of all things. All growth, according to Heraclitus, comes from war. There is a constant life and death struggle in nature, not just within human beings. Tillich views this as a universal condition of existence.

The self-creativity of life involves a process in which one temporarily surrenders one's normal balanced self, grows outwardly becoming imbalanced, finally forming a different balanced self. Toil and struggle that produce this growth are essential and are intertwined with God's curse laid on Adam and Eve in Genesis 3:17: "...cursed is the ground because of you; in toil you shall eat of it all the days of your life." In the Old Testament, the New Testament, and in the early church, value is placed upon toil and struggle but little glorification of it is found in the Bible. This contrasts with the Protestant ethic, industrial society, and socialism. Without toil, work, and struggle, call it what you will, little growth would take place within the life of a human being. This is a major paradox in life.

Self-creativity within the dimension of the spirit—According to Tillich, culture is "that which takes care of something, keeps it alive, and makes it grow. In this way, man can cultivate everything he encounters, but in doing so, he does not leave the cultivated object unchanged; he creates something new from it;"[11] It is for this reason that Tillich exams the following three cultural areas in his discussion of growth through self-creativity in the dimension of the spirit:

1. language and technology,

2. application of theory, and

3. acts of individuals and groups.

1. *Language and technology,* together, produce what is new in culture. Biblically, this partnership is first seen in Genesis 2:15-19, as God requests man and woman to give the animals names (language) and to cultivate the garden (technology).

[11.] Tillich, Vol. III, p. 57.

There are a number of *language* forms of particular significance to the field of theology beginning with: (1) the language of the "here and now" that simply describes occurrences as they are seen, this was perhaps the first language form used by humans, (2) the language of myth, which combines the "here and now" understanding with understandings beyond the "here and now," such as religion and, (3) the language of the poets and the scientists.

Regarding myths, Tillich suggests that any single myth, may be made up of a combination of several religious symbols that, together, provide a particular understanding. Regarding poetic language, it also may use symbols, but uses them in a different manner. It uses sensory images that express meanings impossible to express in any other way.

Within language, whether of the "here and now" or through thoughts beyond one's immediate experience, there is always the problem of personal bias or the inability of the persons being able to understand the communication. According to Tillich, the bias may take a number of forms such as: (1) only one meaning of a particular subject is given even though there maybe many possible meanings; (2) identical language that is understood differently depending on the cultural background of the hearer; (3) a carelessness in expression through an overload of information on the one-hand to withholding information on the other-hand; (4) the manipulation of language for the sake of a purpose not based in reality (such as flattery, argumentation, propaganda, and gossip); and, finally, (5) the deliberate twisting of language to mean something different from the reality itself, through hiding, distorting, and contradicting the actual situation. These problems are present, to some degree, in all language, including the scriptures.

Within the *language of scientific inquiry* there are still more problems. Scientific inquiry involves the recording of repetitious observable and measurable acts, and applying the learning in a manner through what is commonly called a body of scientific knowledge. Presumably scientific knowledge is purged of all problems. It is pure. According to Tillich, however, scientific knowledge is full of ambiguities that can be classified into several different categories, such as: (1) the imperfections in observation that occur because of varying errors or distortions introduced through observer bias; (2) errors made in applying knowledge through processes that are unable to include all relevant information, or which hide facts to make the process fit; (3) problems involved in understanding processes that include partial truths; and (4) problems found in argumentation designed to support certain concepts, having within them undiscussed or unnoticed assumptions which influence the arguments. These are called ideologies when based on one's societal background, and rationalizations when resulting from one's psychological situation, according to Tillich.

Language and technology are closely related, and, together, create what is new in culture. Technology produces tools to be used by humans. There are many problems inherent in this that directly affect the development of humans toward their full potential. For instance, tools allow humans to set and pursue purposes and directions that transcend one's natural environment. In doing this, however, one not only has the potential to gain a better life but may also have the potential to threaten or diminish life.

This ambiguity leads to three different types of problems associated with technology and the production of tools:

1. the problems associated with freedom and limitation,

2. the problems of means and ends, and

3. the problems of self and thing.

(1) The problems associated with *freedom and limitation* are powerfully expressed through both myth and legend. For instance, Adam, in Genesis 2:16, was given the freedom to eat the fruit of all the trees in the garden except the tree of the knowledge of good and evil. Adam ate of this tree and God cursed the land and promised that Adam would

return to dust as a result (Genesis 3:17-19). In the act of eating the apples, there was a creative aspect, the freedom to eat the apples in the garden and there was a destructive aspect, the limitation placed on Adam, "do not eat the apples of the tree of the knowledge of good and evil."

So it is with human beings throughout all of history, most recently illustrated through the harnessing of atomic energy. God gave humans the freedom to explore and use the universe, and, in so doing, provided the means of self-destruction. Awareness of this conflict is voiced by many scientists today who are aware of the destructive possibilities of new scientific knowledge and tools.

(2) The second problem, that of *means and ends*, is related to the first. It differs, however, in the sense of making the limitation concrete. It asks the question: For what? If the "for what" is to satisfy the basic needs of society (such as supplying adequate food, water, healthful conditions, etc.), there is normally little problem in justifying the filling of the need. However, as basic needs are satisfied, new "needs" are identified, they are satisfied, and once satisfied a new regime of needs is created. The production of means—gadgets—becomes an end in itself, as there is no overall superior end identified.

Tillich feels it is this cycle of means and ends that produces the emptiness so evident in many lives today as one searches for meaning and secures just another gadget. Tillich does not suggest, however, that it is possible to simply end the production of more and different goods or tools. It is impossible to say to the scientist: Quit your research! Uncertainties cannot be overcome by stopping creativity.

(3) The third and last problem to be discussed regarding technology is that of *self and thing*. A thing, as defined by Tillich, is that which is produced by technology. A house, a bridge, a train is a thing. Through control of technology humans are able to change or transform natural objects into things (trees into lumber is but one example). As this occurs one loses one's sense of self becoming "things" oriented, losing

much of one's naturalness, one's appreciation for the out-of-doors, of beauty, and one's relationships to others. Society becomes artificial. This process, so evident in many lives, results in one becoming enslaved to one's beautifully furnished home, one's latest model car, and the job or profession within which one works. One cannot annihilate technical production to reduce this ambiguity, any more than a scientist can quit doing research.

   2. *Application of "theoria"*—Being able to theorize is a basic function of culture, and, within the dimension of the spirit, involves examining the world in search of meaning, absorbing into oneself the knowledge gained.[12] There are two primary ways of gaining knowledge in one's search for meaning: (1) through direct experience, and (2) through aesthetic expressions, such as poetry, mythology, art, and music.

   There are problems involved in gathering meaningful information through *direct experience*. How does one know the truth behind what one sees or experiences? Many people believe that nothing is true that can't be proven scientifically. But what about the truths found in religion and philosophy, many of which cannot be proven? Do we need another definition for truth?

   The function of aesthetics is to express qualities of being that can only be understood through the creativity found in art, poetry, myth, music and similar forms of expression. Qualities are expressed in terms of beauty, which in the Greek sense, also means "good." The question arises, however, whether the artistic expression really represents reality or is it lacking in reality? This is a difficult question to answer, as who knows whether it is truly an expression that helps one to better visualize or understand reality, or is it simply an expression of a particular person's limited perception of reality.

---

   12. Tillich uses the Greek "theoria" as he believes the modern form of the word, theory, has lost the meaning and power originally intended.

3. *Acts of individuals and groups*—According to Tillich, the intended aim of a group under the dimension of the Spirit is justice and humanity "....Justice as the fulfillment of the inner aim of social groups and their mutual relations,..." and "...humanity in the sense of the fulfillment of one's inner aim with respect to oneself and one's personal relations in co-ordination with justice."[13] *Within an individual* there exists a gap between the intended aim to develop his/her full potential and what is actually occurring. The goal of one involved in self-creativity is to develop one's full potential. An individual, striving to reach full potential is confronted by a major uncertainty, however, regarding who decides the direction to be taken, the individual or the social group of the individual. If it is the person developing there is an assumption that he/she knows what it means to be totally human. This is not so under the conditions of an estranged existence—it's a case of "the blind leading the blind."

In contrast, the individual involved in a social group, is in danger of becoming an "object" of the group, the direction for a full life being decided by others. This may happen unintentionally whenever two or more people interact, or intentionally in situations of formal education, employee orientation programs, and other areas that involve formal indoctrination. In the extreme, guidance received from a therapist (or a counselor), may result in the person becoming an object, subject to the control of the therapist. This is not the role that a professional therapist would hope to achieve. However, even with the best intentions or professionalism, the values of the therapist, the teacher, or the friend are transferred to the one being helped. There is nothing necessarily bad about this except that one should be aware of the depersonalizing

---

[13.] Paul Tillich, *Systematic Theology* (Chicago: University of Chicago Press, 1963), III, pg. 67.

process that takes place. One is made an object. This should be reduced to the degree possible.

A social group, as a group, grows principally toward justice, rather than growing towards its full potential (including justice) as does an individual. Tillich suggests that social groups attempt to control the relationships between members through rules that are often made into law. Differences within the group are provided for depending on the group's system of justice operating within the group.

Some system of justice is present even when there is a conquering group. Justice given the slave, as an example, is still justice, at least according to the ruling group. This is true, although it may be seen as an injustice at a higher level of viewpoint. Groups, or nations, are often best known by the type of justice they dispense.

The growth of individuals within a strong social group is full of problems and contradictions. If the rules of the group are not fully understood, they can lead to an expectation of some form of utopian society, impossible to achieve. On the other hand, the inability to live up to the rules might lead to an attitude of despair that there is no possibility of real justice. Both of these extreme positions lead to great frustration and anxiety.

Problems and contradictions inherent in the growth of individuals in a social group as it moves toward greater justice may be placed in four distinct categories:

inclusiveness and exclusiveness
competition and equality
leadership, and
humanism

The *first major contradiction* cited involves what Tillich calls *inclusiveness and exclusiveness*. A group, by definition, involves some type of delineation. It may be a society of dentists, doctors, lawyers, a union, a ski club, or the Ford Motor Company. A group, therefore, accepts certain people, and excludes others. The cohesiveness of the group is maintained by its exclusiveness. Inherent within these groups is a center of interest around which the group forms.

The more exclusive the group, according to Tillich, the stronger the center of interest, and the narrower the scope of growth. The situation becomes even more evident, however, when the group moves to increase its cohesiveness by excluding other groups that had previously been included. The larger group may be inclusive of an entire company and a more cohesive group may be only the supervisors and managers within the company. The danger here is growing toward a more limited and exclusive viewpoint represented by the particular aims and concerns of supervisory and managerial personnel. The more exclusive a group becomes the narrower the perspective and the slower the growth of its members.

Conversely, every move of the group that weakens its cohesiveness, increases its array of individuals and groups near its outer boundary. Examples, might include the new worker, the skilled worker, the unskilled worker, in some cases minority group members, or the dissenters. When this occurs one's perspective is changed and the direction of growth broadened.

A *second contradiction*, according to Tillich, in the application of justice involves *competition and equality*. Competition between individuals is a way of life in family relations, business, social relations, the struggle for political power, intellectual creativity, as well as other areas. There is a competitive striving for dominance, followed by a moment of unity, and away we go again, toward more competition. There is almost a continuous spirit of competition within groups of all kinds, which most often involves winning or losing.

Within this competitive framework, many inequalities between people become evident, particularly in relationship to equality under the law. Under the law, a fully mature person and one who is mentally ill have the same legal rights. However, in practice, there is a major inconsistency. There are many instances of the depersonalizing and demeaning of the mentally ill, the disabled, ethnic minorities and women. The list is long and reaches into every avenue of life.

According to Tillich, not only are there some important inconsistencies within the application "equality under the law," but there is an inequality within competition itself. The competitive process may deny the right of people with the highest qualifications for leadership to be leaders according to their ability, resulting in devastating consequences for those needing effective leadership. An example of this, is a competitive processes that selects individuals based on personality traits only, rather than on total qualifications.

It may deny the opportunity for maximizing growth to those most able to respond to challenges which stimulate their growth. As an example, a poor person with the highest of potential finds it more difficult to go to college, or to move to areas of the country where there is greater opportunity, than those financially better off who have less potential.

It may also result in those with the highest potential being held back from developing their potential while, at the same time, demanding from those with less potential, performances that are excessive and result in failure. All of society would suffer if individuals where treated as though they all had equal abilities and potential. They do not. The most that can be hoped for is equal justice under the law, however, the examples cited above make this something of a utopian ideal not based on reality.

The *third contradiction* identified by Tillich, is that of *leadership*. Leadership is involved in all human relationships, from the parent-child to the ruler-subject. Within the many forms of leadership there are differing styles, some of which result in the highest form of creativity from the leaders, to those that are totally dominated by one or a few leaders, and has no opportunity to exercise creativity.

Perhaps the most obvious misapplication of the leadership function involves that which comes from power struggles involving different degrees of strength and the drive of the stronger to enslave the weaker. This, as far as Tillich is concerned, is an abuse of the principle of leadership and not its essence. True leadership, as Tillich sees it, involves a leadership through which self- integration and self-creativity within the group are possible. Individuals are encouraged to use their natural spontaneity and creativity in pursuing the aim of the group. Leadership is needed only in order to provide a united effort.

In the absence of leadership a group could be united only through some form of psychological mass movement in which spontaneity and freedom of the individual are lost—there being no room for independent decision. Examples include propagandists of all types who try to produce mass movements, not only in the political but also within the advertising realm. They do not necessarily want to be leaders, but to be instigators or managers of a mass movement. The possibility of using the power of leadership to transform mature individuals into a mass movement within which everyone thinks alike is frightening to Tillich.

Ideally, a leader represents the power and justice of the group as well as representing the power and justice of the leader. This applies not only to the leader as an individual, but also applies to the power and justice systems from which the leader came. This situation is a source of difficulty when the leader applies his or her individual ideology to the social group being lead. This is true for all social groups no matter whether the power exercised is that of a dictator, an aristocracy, or a congress. This is also true of voluntary groups. Attempts at removing leadership or authority figures are often self defeating as they lead to anarchy and chaos; a power vacuum is formed which is most often filled by a dictator.

A *fourth contradiction, humanism,* is the product or aim of the group as its culture is formed by the development of the individuals within the group. It is important to ask the question then: Does the development of humanity's potential have an ultimate aim? Is there a universe of meaning which may contain the ultimate aim of all humanity? The answer to these question is in two parts: first, in terms of the total universe, and second, exclusively within the human realm.

In the sense of a total universe, Tillich says, yes, there is a universe of meaning which is the collective development of all the potential in the universe. This includes matter, beginning with the subatomic, the subatomic through the atom, the atom through the molecule, the molecule through plants and animals, and, finally, culminating in the highest form of being, humans.

Regarding the human realm, a spirit is present only in humans, and the ultimate meaning of the universe can only be found in the spirit. This is the basis of the humanistic idea, the basis of culture, and the justification for humanistic philosophy. The word humanism, according to Tillich, refers to the intrinsic aim of all cultural activity within which humanity is engaged. It includes within it the concept of a humanity that values kindness and benevolence, also providing for the total fulfillment of one's life within the concepts of justice and truth. Humanism embraces these concepts, developing them throughout all of humanity's cultural activities (as in families, religious institutions, in language, education, and the arts).

There are several problems involved in humanism. First of all, it disregards religion as an overarching entity that influences all cultural activities. Instead, religion is perceived as only one of many cultural activities within the self-creativity process, with little effect on other cultural activities.

A second problem has to do with education. "Educating" means providing new information and behaviors presumably leading toward some final goal not necessarily fully understood. A purely humanistic response to this, according to Tillich, is toward the full development of a human being according to each individual's potential. However, since the distance is so great between the many possibilities for growth of the individual and what is ultimately possible, given enough time, the humanistic view would have to include the statement "within the life span of the individual." According to Tillich, this is a fatal qualification, as it eliminates the possibility of humanism's ideal of providing the final answer to the educational and general cultural question: What is the aim of cultural activity? The aim would be beyond the life span of the individual.

Perhaps of greater importance is humanism's exclusion of the vast majority of people from its ideal of an educational process that results in the full development of one's potential. Under either autocratic or democratic systems of education, the vast majority of individuals are secluded from higher forms of culture and educational depth. Education simply "takes" differently between one individual and another. A major problem of humanistic education is its isolation of individuals and groups best able to progress educationally from the masses of average people. In doing this, it diminishes the possibility of forming an ideal community open to all people, which is an essential ideal of humanism. The more successful humanistic education is, the greater the differences between individuals. These differences increase the difficulties involved in creating a community open to everyone.

The Self-transcendence of Life: Problems

The third and last step in reaching one's potential is self-transcendence. Self-transcendence is the process of movement toward God. It cannot be measured as in science, or through direct, observable experiences. It is a matter of one's inner consciousness.

The Apostle Paul, in his letter to the Roman Church (Romans 8:19-22), speaks to the longing within people to be freed from the "subjection to futility" and "the shackles of mortality." In other words, people yearn for the freedom to rise above the realities of the existing, transcending life as it is known to a God of ultimate and infinite being. The philosopher Aristotle calls this the search for an "unmoved mover"—a mover beyond our current existence.

The greatness of life—According to Tillich, one who works at being great, does so at inordinate risk, as it requires a behavior that differs dramatically from the norms of society. In the case of Jesus there was a serious consequence. His greatness resulted in his death on the cross. The tragedy, of course, was overcome by his resurrection.

It is God's intent that individuals strive for greatness of life through a transcendence that rises above their normal existence. The drive for greatness has been expressed by poets, painters, and philosophers through the ages. Its inviolability is seen initially in Genesis 1:26 when God addresses the creation of the first man and woman:

> *Let us make man/woman in our image, after our likeness; and let them have dominion over the fish of the sea, and over the birds of the air, and over the cattle, and over all the earth, and over every creeping thing that creeps upon the earth.*

It is clear, according to Tillich, that God's will that people seek greatness is not realized when one's life is dominated by smallness of thought, a fear of reaching out to the new, and the willingness to accept the status quo, no matter how unjust.

Greatness and tragedy—According to Tillich, tragic circumstances that often accompany greatness are inevitable. One only needs to review history to discover this—the assassination of many of the world's great leaders.

Unfortunately, according to Tillich, many people in their striving for greatness fall into the trap of hubris. In their striving they become their own god, becoming arrogantly possessive, often believing themselves above the law. Too often the result is the destruction of others as well as their own self-destruction. An unfortunate part of this is that they fail to see the destructive path they have taken. It is this type of behavior on the part of the powerful, according to Tillich, that the Old Testament Prophets spent so much time speaking out against.

According to Tillich, if greatness is inevitably connected with tragedy, it is natural that people should try to avoid tragedy by avoiding greatness. This, of course, is an unconscious process, but, nevertheless, very common among many people. It may be seen in the reluctance of many of this nation's best people to run for political office, or the lack of interest by many in filling difficult but important jobs. Not seeking important leadership roles is a way to avoid tragedy through avoiding greatness. This, however, results in humans denying their ultimate potential for development.

The role of religion—Religion is a special function of life in the dimension of the spirit, and as such, has many problems associated with it. Many of the problems, although natural, are very difficult to resolve. Religion can lead the institution of the church to the highest expression of greatness possible, striving to become spiritually perfect and pure in its greatness, and, at the same time, religion can lead the church toward the most secularized institution on earth with the search for greatness substantially destroyed. These two directions are always present somewhere within the totality of the church as it exists at any one time. This problem is observable in all of history, and is of great concern to many people today.

One of the first problems that religion confronts in its striving for a transcendent greatness is the presence of secularized aspects in every religious act. Tillich discusses this by addressing: (1) the church and organized religion as institutions, and (2) the reduction of religion to the level of culture.

(1) The *institutionalization of the organized church and religion*, has resulted in a church often more interested in the secular than tran-

scending to the infinite, God. It does this by performing a set of pre-scribed activities, espousing a set of stated doctrines, becoming a social pressure group, or a political power.

Critics concentrate their criticism of the church and organized reli-gion on these external trappings—the dogma, the social groups, or the political action. When they do so, however, they fail to see through these outward manifestations into the inner self-transcendent, great, and holy character found internally in most churches. This is unfortunate, according to Tillich, as the total nature of the church is eclipsed by these outer manifestations. Not only is the totality of what is happening in the church eclipsed, but in many instances, unfortunately, the social groups or dogma provide the direction that the inner, personal lives of members take, secularizing them as well. In some forms of organized religion the magnitude of this "shaping" is overwhelming as far as Tillich is concerned. One does not have to go far to find examples of secularization. Perhaps the most obvious is the often overriding atten-tion paid to the church's mortgage, its financial health, or the preserva-tion of its cathedrals and golden icons.

According to Tillich, the secular institutions of the church influence the inner life of the members, preventing a totally transcendent holiness; it is also true that the holiness within the inner life of the members influ-ences the direction taken by the secular institutions, moving the church toward pure transcendent holiness. In essence, it is a "mixed bag." No one should draw premature conclusions about organized religion due to some of its perceived, as well as actual pettiness. The pettiness found in a church is no argument against its elements of greatness. Greatness and pettiness may be present in the same institution, as they are combined in even the greatest of people.

(2) The *reduction of religion to the level of culture* is viewed by many people as a major problem. According to Tillich, religion is often seen as a creation of culture with no self-transcending aspects. It is perceived as an interesting and perhaps necessary part of culture, playing its role

within the life of the individual or social institutions much like other aspects of culture. Religion is explained away as a product of psychological or sociological sources and considered an illusion, or at best, an ideology. According to Tillich, this view is reinforced by religious education that oftentimes does not address the mystery of God or of being, to which religion is thought to address itself. Religious education, instead, too often concentrates on the pragmatics of life as experienced in daily life.

A second major problem within the reduction of religion to the level of culture involves the relationship between the divine and the demonic. The divine is that which is God's. The demonic is that which distorts humanity. According to Tillich, demonization of the religious occurs in every religion, every day, sometimes consciously, most frequently subconsciously. Whenever those in the church truly believe they are nearing the divine sphere, the demonic appears. Perhaps the best example of this in recent history occurred within the Roman Empire, "…whose greatness, dignity, and sublime character was universally acknowledged, but which became demonically possessed when it vested itself with divine holiness and reduced the split which led to the antidemonic struggle of Christianity and the demonic persecution of the Christians…."[14]

Students of religious history can see this process occurring continuously in all of the great religions, as they take on more and more power in the name of the "one truth," as they define the truth. Too often, religion fails to recognize or resist this problem. In a little broader sense, religion itself, is involved in demonization as it establishes rigid religious structures designed to represent what it says is holy. The act of making liturgical practices or moral positions holy, is a demonic act.

[14.] Tillich, III, p.103.

When this occurs it rejects all criticism raised in the name of justice, defending itself in the name of holiness. Criticism is not tolerated.

The divine-demonic split, according to Tillich, is also seen in the realm of personal life through the idea of sainthood. Most often saints are identified based on their negative, ascetic traits that, within the church, constitute saintliness. This results in "guilt-trips" within those who do not live the life of a saint, and it denies the full development of one's greatness. The goal of sainthood is reached through an act of ascetism, rather than fulfillment, which is an act of faith.

Dogma also plays an important role in preserving the traditions of the past—the true importance of this should not be overlooked. However, dogma, in too many instances, is used as an instrument of control by the church, effectively preventing new revelations or approaches to the self- transcendent. This is done when those in religious authority suppress new insights in the name of dogma (tradition), or a truth more recently consecrated or made "holy" by the church.

THE SEARCH FOR A LIFE FREE OF PROBLEMS

Only within three important religious symbols can a life free of problems be visualized: the divine Spirit, the Kingdom of God, and Eternal Life. Outside of these three representations, all of life is a mix of goodness and sinfulness that, together, produce the many ambiguities and problems found in life.

Within these three symbols, a life of perfect goodness and greatness may be found. The divine Spirit is the presence of God within us. The Kingdom of God, is the final fulfillment toward which we are moving. Eternal Life is one's defeat of the limits of time and space, including the present existence on earth.

Commentary

Tillich relies heavily on the discoveries of science, of historical analysis, and other disciplines in his systematics theology. He does so fully aware, however, of their limitations in the search for truth. Sir John Eccles, Nobel Laureate in medicine and physiology, expresses Tillich's concern well, when he tells us that we need to discredit the belief that science will ultimately deliver to us the final truth. Although science may probe some of the deepest mysteries of the universe—discovering some—it will never explain values, beauty, love, friendship or literary quality. Those scientists who believe that someday they will be able to do so are peddling superstition. Science will also never be able to explain the uniqueness of each individual, or answer such questions as: Who am I? Why am I here? What happens after death? As "these are all mysteries that are beyond science."[15]

---

15. Sir John Eccles, "Science Can't Explain Who Am I? Why Am I Here?" *U.S. News and World Report*, (December, 1984), p. 80.

Some people believe, or seem to believe, that nothing is true that cannot be proven scientifically. They overlook the fact that we are just beginning on our scientific pursuits, much more is yet to be discovered than has been discovered to date. Metaphorically speaking, one may think of an island in the Pacific Ocean as representing all that has been proven scientifically to date, and the Pacific Ocean representing the knowledge that lies ahead, yet to be understood. As the island expands in size, the vast size of the ocean becomes even more evident. It is there, but the mysteries within it have yet to be discovered. Projecting outward from the island into the mysteries of the ocean is the role of symbol, poetry, of music and the visual arts, of mythology, of theology, and of religious faith. These are the instruments with which we look ahead. They are not in conflict with science. They enrich scientific discovery, at times addressing realms of human concern that science may never be able to probe.

There may or may not be a providential God who provides direction to the universe as well as to individuals as they enter into the mysteries of the "ocean." We really don't know for sure. It is apparent, however, that there are some universal laws (God's laws) that we continue to discover and expand upon, which when followed produce for the individual a fullfilment and meaningfulness far beyond what often seems possible. Many have discovered this. Most do not know how to relate this experience to others. Yet it is real.[16]

---

16. Richard M. Pomeroy, *In Search of Meaning*, (Berkeley: Glen Berkeley Press, 1991, p. 24.

Discussion

1. Is the dimension of the spirit found only in humans? Is there the possibility of additional dimensions beyond that of the spirit?

2. Discuss your understanding of: (1) self-integration, (2) self-creativity, and (3) self-transcendence? Share some personal experiences of growth, in each of the three processes of growth described by Tillich.

3. Is maximum growth within humans dependent upon adversity?

4. Do you agree that the "highest" form of life is the human being? How about the most "valuable" form of life?

5. What does Tillich mean when he talks about a moral imperative to join affirmatively with all persons in spite of their difference? What is the practical application of this in your life?

6. How is the church similar to other institutions? How is it different? Does the church need a major reformation today? What might this look like?

7. Is the church fairly and accurately represented in today's news media? If not, what action should the churches be taking to correct the situation? What might you do?

CHAPTER 4

The Divine Spirit

Chapter Introduction

The divine Spirit resides within the spirit of all human beings, providing them the power to develop their potential within God's love. Tillich is uncomfortable with the emphasis that is so often placed on the power of the divine Spirit in producing miracles. He believes that the divine Spirit's power is much more important in providing meaning and direction to one's life.

Tillich discusses the role of the Word and the Sacraments as the media through which the divine Spirit communicates with the Spiritual Community. He refers to Spiritual Communities, rather than the church, as a Spiritual Community is found both inside and outside the church in youth alliances, civic, and even political groups. These latter ones he calls the "latent" Spiritual Community.

The Divine Spirit and the Human Spirit

The divine Spirit—As far as we know, the dimension of the spirit is present only in human beings and is that which provides meaning to life. According to Tillich, it is within the human spirit that the divine Spirit is found. Those who acknowledge this presence are empowered by the divine Spirit in their search for an ever closer relationship with God who is the source of all goodness.

Although Tillich believes strongly in the presence of the divine Spirit within all human beings, he is troubled by what often appears to be a concentration on the "outer trappings" of the divine Spirit's presence. Individuals are reportedly "grabbed up" into moments of ecstasy, able to speak in "tongues" that they have never been able to speak in before, similar to what happened to the apostles at Pentecost:

> And suddenly a sound came from heaven like the rush of a mighty wind, and it filled all the house where they were sitting. And there appeared to them tongues as of fire, distributed and resting on each one of them. And they were all filled with the Holy Spirit and began to speak in other tongues, as the Spirit gave them utterance. (Acts 2:2-4)

When this occurs, individuals often report "miraculous" occurrences in their lives. In many instances, they report having been healed of an incurable disease. Tillich questions whether these "miracles" are real, as there is no rational explanation for their occurrence. He does not reject their possibility, however, as they are wide spread and some may have substance to them yet undiscovered.

He cites a number of miraculous instances in the Bible such as a person being transferred bodily from one place to another, the raising of Lazarus from the dead (John 1:40-44), the immediate healing of both the body and the mind (Luke 9:10-11), and a knowledge of strange tongues (Acts 2:4). These stories to Tillich are symbols of theological truth and, as such, have great meaning. If taken literally, natural law must have been overcome through the direct intervention of the divine Spirit. As stated before, Tillich doubts that the divine Spirit operates in this way.

Regardless of whether miracles, in fact, occur, Tillich is uncomfortable with the emphasis that is so often placed on the power of the divine Spirit in producing them. He believes that the divine Spirit is much more important in providing meaning and direction to one's life.

The Word and the Sacraments: language—According to Tillich, the-ological tradition defines the Word and the Sacraments as an important means through which the divine Spirit exercises its power, the Word (in particular the Gospels), and the Sacraments, being the visible signs of God's love for humans. Though Tillich accepts this tradition, he does so with the understanding that the power of the divine Spirit is one of par-ticipativeness and influence, rather than one of orchestrating miracu-lous events.

Sacraments—There are only two Sacraments recognized by Protestantism, the Lord's Supper (Communion) and Baptism. Many more Sacraments are recognized in Catholicism than is true in the Protestant church. According to Tillich, the term "sacramental" needs to be freed up from the limited view of various religious groups. There are groups who believe that sacraments should not be a part of religious life. Others limit the Sacraments to two, five, or seven specific types of acts. A debate among religious groups through the years has often cen-tered on what is the appropriate ritual that, when done, becomes a magic that "saves the recipient into eternity." This is without any refer-ence to the faith of the recipient.

There must be, according to Tillich, a larger understanding of the meaning and application of what is a sacramental act. Sacraments, looked at in a broader sense, may include everything in which the divine Spirit has been experienced without limitation on specific types and numbers.

Language—Language is fundamental to all cultural functions and is the Spirit's most important medium. Tillich suggests that the language found in the Bible, however:

> *…does not contain the words (language) of God, but it can and in a unique way has become the Word of God. Its uniqueness resides in the fact that it is the document of the central revelation (of God), with respect to both its giving (from God) and receiving*

(by the writers of the scriptures) sides. Every day, by its impact on people inside and outside the church, the Bible proves that it is the Spirit's most important medium in the Western tradition. But it is not the only medium, . . [17]

Tillich enlarges indefinitely the number of words that can become the Word of God. If a specific set of words transmit the Spirit of God all religious and cultural documents, the whole of human literature, even that which is average or small, including the spoken word in sermon or in ordinary conversation may be the Word of God.

The question naturally arises as to how one distinguishes the "true" word of God from the many competing and contradictory words whose proponent's claim they are "the" Word of God? Tillich responds that nothing is the Word of God if it contradicts the faith and love as recorded in the Bible. Biblical faith and love are the works of the New Being as revealed through Jesus the Christ. They are the ultimate criteria.

One of the major questions regarding the Bible is its relationship with what is called the "inner" word. Many Spirit-Movements, from the earliest days of Christianity down through the centuries to the present time, have challenged the primacy of the Bible and church authorities. Many in the Spirit Movement felt that the "inner word" within oneself is just as authoritative, perhaps more so. Following the Protestant Reformation of the sixteenth century, which liberated some religious groups from the Pope, a number of religious groups desired liberation from the literal application of the Bible and creeds as well. The position taken was that since the divine Spirit is "God present within the person," religious belief is not dependent upon God's past revelations, including those revelations contained in the Bible and Sacraments. To them, the revelation in the Bible and Sacraments are superseded by a

---

[17.] Tillich, III, p. 124.

God who dwells in the depths of the individual speaking through the "inner word." The "outer word" is no longer needed.

Tillich is greatly influenced by the inner Spirit-movement as it is free from the rigidity of dogma and rituals found in many churches. He is critical, however, of the totality of the "break." As far as Tillich is concerned, it is the inner word that, rather than superseding the past, makes the past relevant to today.

Given the power of the "inner word" it is evident that words are essential to a communication between God and humans. Even the thinking mind thinks in words as ideas are formed and understood through combinations of words. Humans remember and record into meaningful wholes that which has been spoken in the past. The speeches and writings of the prophets and mystics and all those claiming divine inspirations are put into words (language) representing their respective traditions, yet pointing toward God. God when communicating with the prophets of the Bible, did not give them new facts about the past, present, or future, he provided them, instead, the ability to interpret the facts in terms of ultimate meanings, speaking out in the language and culture of their time.

According to Tillich, when those in the Spirit-movement received the "inner word" in their language, they too were instructed by God to put it in terms of their experiences (using their language, the same as the prophets were instructed). The ultimate meaning of the facts are the same, it is the language that differs.

Insights gained through the "inner word," particularly during the Reformation, revealed a Church bound by religious ambiguity within its tradition. The Church was not responding to the social situation of the lowest classes of society. The Spirit needed to work within the life of the individual, rather than simply the church. As a result, the Spirit-movements have led to many Christian social movements in the last centuries, often referred to as the "social gospel."

Come, O blessed of my Father, inherit the kingdom prepared for you from the foundation of the world; for I was hungry and you gave me food, I was thirsty and you gave me drink, I was a stranger and you welcomed me, I was naked and you clothed me, I was sick and you visited me, I was in prison and you came to me.... (Matthew 25:34-36)

Faith and love—According to Tillich, the divine Spirit interacts with the human spirit through faith and love. Faith, according to Tillich (deliberately defining it narrowly), is the state of a human who is enveloped by the divine Spirit (an admittedly narrow definition); love is defined as that which moves one closer to God (as seen through one's works). Faith and love are interdependent as "...faith without works is dead." (Jas 2:26b)

Faith, in a broader sense than used above, may be defined both formally and religiously. Formally, it is a situation within which all people find themselves as they look for some ultimate meaning or value no matter how worthy or unworthy it may be, i.e., God, money, power, good works, or status. Faith, in a religious sense, is defined by Tillich as the leading of a life empowered by the divine Spirit (New Being) and divorced from all ambiguity. These definitions contrast with the distorted view of faith as that which is hard to believe, that which is not proven, or in believing absurdities and nonsense.

According to Tillich, religious faith has three component parts: (1) regeneration, (2) justification, and (3) sanctification. Regeneration acknowledges the power of the divine Spirit (New Being) working within one's life, justification acknowledges the acceptance of this power by the individual, even though one's life remains full of sinfulness, and sanctification acknowledges that one's life is moving toward God through faith and love.

Love, as Tillich uses it here, is called agape love, which stands for God's perfect love and is not experienced by humans without the presence of the divine Spirit. It can be seen through the love that one has for one's "neighbor" which overcomes all differences that might separate neighbor from neighbor. Agape love is the character of the divine life itself and is the love God has for all of humanity. When people begin to love God as God loves them, they are loving one another in agape. This is a very important one-two relationship.

Love, separate from God, is usually thought of as a purely emotional state. According to Tillich, this is a very limited view, as love is a part of all the functions of life with its roots in the very center of one's being. Within an exclusively emotional love, however, relationships always include a degree of strife between the persons involved in the relationship, each person demanding something from the other. An exclusively emotional love is not strong enough to overcome this. It can be overcome only through the will to unite, as in agape love.

Agape love overcomes the problems and ambiguities of other kinds of love involved in friendships and sexual desire. It provides a completeness not otherwise possible. It has this power through three separate but interdependent qualities: the one loved is accepted without restrictions or conditions, the love continues in spite of what the loved one might do, and the love provides completeness not otherwise possible with the one that is loved.

Tillich concludes by telling us that the path toward God is full of greatness, dignity, and holiness, though in partnership with the divine Spirit, and is fraught with estrangement and sin as well. This is true with minister and lay person alike—it is not a pure path, it is a mixed path. It is a mark of religious maturity to understand this.

The Divine Spirit in the World

The New Being and its presence in history—According to Tillich, the divine Spirit and its creation, the New Being, have been active throughout history. They are constantly at work assisting human beings in their search for God and their struggle for a more fulfilling life. Although the New Being and divine Spirit are a part of this struggle, how this occurs is difficult to fully understand. This is so because to possess a New Being does not make one entirely free of sinful ways.

Regarding the divine Spirit's presence in other than the Christian, Tillich tells us that there was an early "manna" religion in the Polynesian culture that emphasized the divine Spirit in the "depth" of everything that is. The manna religion was invisible, mysterious, approachable only through definite rituals that are known only to the priests. This early vision of the divine Spirit is present within all major religions though with many different variations.

The mythologies of Greece and India, which separate the ruling divine powers from the existing world, also find parallels in all the major religions. Tillich is concerned about attempts to discount this mythology. Looking at it as though it was literally true leads many people to discount it, consequently overlooking its symbolism. We must understand its symbolic importance as it represents humanity's attempt at describing religious meaning and the presence of the divine Spirit. Early religions, such as those found in Persia, or in Manicheism, fought against the potential demonization of the divine Spirit's purity. To a very large degree they concentrated all that is pure in one figure, the divine, and all that is impure, or demonic, in another. This was not an ultimately successful approach, although it is obvious how it has influenced late Judaism and Christianity, both of which often overlook the combination of saint and sinner in people.

According to Tillich, the two most important examples of the presence of the divine Spirit in other than Christianity appear in Asian and European mysticism, and the monotheism (one God) of Judaism. In the latter, it includes religions based on Judaism, such as that of the Muslim and Christian faiths. Mysticism perceives the divine Spirit as above the world, as in the mythology of Greece, and yet entering the various functions of life found in the world. Life is lifted up a "spiritual staircase" to the ultimate reality of God. The power of the divine Spirit is experienced, in particular, when all the "steps on the stairway" have been left behind and the mind is grasped with ecstasy.

It is at the point of ultimate reality that two of the world's great religions differ. Hinduism (not so in Buddhism) believes that the ultimate reality involves a "formless self" as its aim. In Christianity, however, the ultimate reality, rather than being formless, involves a "preservation of the individual self." According to Christianity, God does not eliminate the individual but, instead, takes hold of an individual's mind, raising it to unparalleled heights as with the Prophets. The Synoptic Gospels (Matthew, Mark, and Luke) provide an early Christian tradition of this based upon Jesus' total possession by the divine Spirit. According to these Gospels, Jesus was caught-up by the Spirit at the moment of baptism. This confirmed Jesus as the "Son of God."

Regarding ecstatic experiences, they appear repeatedly in the Gospel stories. The divine Spirit sends Jesus into the desert and leads him through a series of temptations. At the same time, it gives him the power of God in respect to people and events, and makes him the conqueror of demons and the healer of mind and body.

Jesus as the Christ, is the ultimate qualitative example of the fullness of the divine Spirit, according to Tillich. As such, qualitatively, all future revelation will not exceed that revealed through Jesus.

The divine Spirit and the Spiritual Community—The Spiritual Community is defined by Tillich, as those people taken up by the New Being, enabling them to overcome the ambiguities found in religion. He uses the term Spiritual Community rather than Church (although many people in churches are taken up by the New Being), for two reasons: (1) the ambiguities and secularization found in the organized Church, as previously discussed, and (2) the Spiritual Community is also found outside the church. The Spiritual Community is hidden, yet very real. It is hidden, however, only in the sense that it cannot be seen, understood, or experienced by those of no faith. This is due to the absence of the New Being in their life.

The story of Pentecost powerfully emphasizes the character of the Spiritual Community. On the day of Pentecost, which occurred 50 days after the resurrection of Jesus, the Apostles became filled with the Holy Spirit "And suddenly a sound came from heaven like the rush of a mighty wind, and it filled the whole house where they were sitting..." Acts 2:2 According to Tillich, the story of Pentecost, whatever its historical accuracy, symbolically includes five very important elements that are critical to the full understanding of the Spiritual Community.

The first element is the rapture or ecstasy that accompanied the experience. This was ecstasy and rational behavior combined, and was the beginning of the Spiritual Community. Without this combination of rationality and ecstasy, within an aura of faith and love, there would be no Spiritual Community.

The second element in the story of Pentecost is the ability of faith to overcome all adversity. The Apostles, during the period between the death of Jesus and the day of Pentecost, were anything but members of the Spiritual Community. The 24th chapter of Luke tells us how the disciples, during the period before the Pentecost, were frightened and dispirited and they "knew him (Jesus) not." They became a part of the Spiritual Community only after Pentecost, when they re-established a faith that overcame their doubt. Without faith there is no Spiritual Community.

The third element is the creation of a love that expresses itself immediately in service to others, especially the poor. Without a love such as this, there is no Spiritual Community.

The fourth element in the story of Pentecost involves unity. The divine Spirit united individuals, nationalities, and traditions together. The disciple's ability to speak various languages (never before understood by them), is symbolic of how the divine Spirit overcomes the disunity within humans symbolized in the story of the Tower of Babel.

Come, let us go down, and there confuse their language, that they may not understand one another's speech. So the Lord scattered them abroad from there over the face of all the earth... (Genesis 11:7-8)

There is no Spiritual Community without a unity of purpose between its parts, although individual cultural differences may vary considerably.

The fifth element in the story of Pentecost is the creation of universality. This is seen in the missionary drive of those grasped by the divine Spirit—they must tell the story of the Gospel, that proclaims the Spiritual Community that is open to all individuals, no matter their sex, race, sexual orientation, culture, and economic and social status. This must be accompanied by an actual desire to include them. Unfortunately, this does not always occur.

The Spiritual Community—The Spiritual Community comes from the reality of Jesus as the Christ, as does the church, yet it is not the church.

Many groups through the centuries have been materially influenced by the divine Spirit, yet have not been a part of the church. They may have, in fact, opposed the church or any other form of religious expression. They may be found among various youth alliances, friendship groups, civic clubs, educational, artistic and even political groups. What, than, is the difference between these groups and the church? The important difference is that in the organized church there is the added dimension of an awareness of and openness to the influence of the divine Spirit and the ultimate unity that God represents. Thus the church, subject to a greater influence by the divine Spirit, has an added ability to resist and overcome the secularization and sinfulness of the world. The church is not always successful in this, as we well know. The record of the Old Testament Prophets, and the 15th Century Protestant

Reformation, however, are two examples of the church's ability to reform itself. It has not lost this capacity.

Given this distinction, Tillich asserts that those movements that exhibit the influence of the divine Spirit, are a part of what he calls a latent or dormant Spiritual Community. Examples include all of Judaism, Islam, Buddhism, communities worshiping the great mythological gods, and the ancient Greek Philosophical schools. The impact of the divine Spirit, and therefore the Spiritual Community, is in all of these and many others.

It must be re-emphasized, according to Tillich, that the Spiritual Community is latent in these groups, and the faith and love of Jesus the Christ is essentially unknown. The love of Christ has not overtly appeared to them, whether they existed before or after his appearance on this earth. However, through inner renewal, transformation, and, or reformation, they unconsciously move closer to the Christ. This is true though they may reject him as he is presented through the preaching and actions of the Christian Churches. Though they may reject the Church, they may represent the Spiritual Community better than many churches.

According to Tillich, these individuals and groups outside of the Christian Church, the latent members of the Spiritual Community, are not complete strangers in "total darkness," as some churches might perceive them. Their membership in the Spiritual Community should serve as a powerful weapon against religious arrogance. Latent or realized (manifest), the Spiritual Community is created by the divine Spirit with its perfect reality seen in Jesus the Christ.

There are two qualities inherent in the Spiritual Community, that deserve special attention. They serve as the criteria by which one may recognize the presence of the Spiritual Community, as well as for judging the church. Of great importance is the Spiritual Communities manifestation as a community of faith. Within this community, the faith of individual members varies and there is a tension between individual faith and the faith of the community as a whole; however, this tension does not lead to breaks as it sometimes does in a church. As a true community of faith, it can overcome all differences through the power and unity found through the divine Spirit.

A second quality is that of holiness and of love. Through love, the Spiritual Community participates in the holiness or sacredness of the divine life, and it gives holiness to the communities within which it is present. This love is imperfect, although it is directed toward the perfect love of God. God's love provides the power needed for a unity of purpose even though there is great diversity between individuals and groups. This is true, no matter the sex, age, race, nation, tradition, and character. The Spiritual Community, in faith, love, and unity moves toward the Kingdom of God, its ultimate fulfillment. Although it moves toward the Kingdom of God, it is not the Kingdom of God.

Commentary

Tillich addresses the subject of estrangement and secularization within the church. He believes that the church not only deserves to be criticized but needs criticism in a constructive and forthright manner. He believes that the church can profit from this criticism as a means of purging itself from its secularized institutions, its legalism, and reliance on sacraments, doctrines and emotions. He suggests that the church falls far short of Christ's Kingdom, as do its individual members. There is a major problem in the church's efforts toward renewal, that strongly interferes with renewal, namely the conflict of interest on the part of many church members with the church's mission. This is particularly true in the church's prophetic voice designed to speak out against institutions of injustice as did the Prophets of the Old Testament. The institutions of injustice and oppression are often composed of church members.

This has been a major problem through the centuries as the state, beginning with the Roman Emperor Constantine, tried to shape the direction to be taken by the church. The state shaped the church to meet its own needs, including the creation of national religions in many countries, in part to protect the status quo. The prophetic voice of the church was muffled.[18]

For the most part, these times are in the past, yet many individual church members continue to give their primary allegiance to specific economic or political institutions. The state continues to be paramount in their mind. Perhaps this is why a poll taken by George Gallup found that "Americans talk a better religion game than they play" as poll results showed a Christian population behaviorally the same as the non-Christian population. Only 10% of those avowing a belief in Christianity behaved in a decidedly more Christian manner.

Discussion

1. What is the relationship between the participation of the divine Spirit in the spiritual and personal development of an individual, in ecstatic experiences, such as those that occurred at Pentecost, and in producing miracles? Do you have a problem with "outer trappings" of the divine Spirit? Do you believe in miracles that overcome the natural laws of the world?

2. How does Tillich address the relationship between revelation, as contained in the Bible, and the "inner word?" Do you believe that revelation continues today, with the same message, but in a more understandable and meaningful language?

3. Do you agree with Tillich's definition of faith?

---

18. Pomeroy, p.76.

4. Can you identify the reality of God's (agape) love in your life? Is it possible to experience this without the presence of God? Within atheists and agnostics?

5. What does Tillich mean when he suggests that it is a mark of religious maturity to recognize that the lives of ministers and lay persons alike are subject to estrangement and sin?

6. As a part of one's ultimate reality, is the preservation of one's "individual self" versus a "formless self" an important part of your religious belief?

7. Do you believe that the many "faces" of the Christian religion today is a problem? If so, how might the church become more unified?

CHAPTER 5

Life And The Divine Spirit

Chapter Introduction

Tillich begins this chapter by addressing one of the paradoxes of the church. The church has two sides, its spiritual side and its institutional side, the latter being the one most visible to society and the one which receives most of the judgement. Although Tillich believes that this judgment should take place, it should not fail to include a judgement of the spiritual side as well.

Tillich probes the nature of the spiritual side of the church (the Spiritual Community) ascribing to it several characteristics, its holiness, its unity and its universality. This side of the church is generally not seen or understood by the average lay person.

Much of the remaining part of the chapter analyzes the problems within the functions of the church and the role of the divine Spirit in their resolution through a theonomous culture.

The Divine Spirit and Life's Problems

The Spiritual Community and the church—The "Spiritual Community" is not a group that exists beside other groups, but rather a power within religious as well as other communities or groups. If a religious community is based on Jesus as the Christ, it is called a church. If it is based on other than the Christ it is not a church. It may be a synagogue, temple congregation, mystery group, monastic group, cult group, or other religious movement.

In religious groups, other than the Christian church, the Spiritual Community is latent or dormant in regard to the specific group's knowledge of the faith and love of Jesus the Christ. Tillich believes very firmly, however, that the divine Spirit is within all individuals whether its presence is acknowledged or not. It is effective in its hidden power within all groups that have as their focus the search for some form of ultimate meaning; it does not have to be Christian in orientation. This is an important distinction.

Collectively, individual churches, in unity through the Christ, are called by Tillich the "church universal." According to Tillich, the church universal (also the individual churches that make up the church universal), may be regarded in two different ways. The church universal is seen as "the body of Christ,"—a spiritual reality—and, simultaneously, as a social group of individual Christians. As the "body of Christ," the churches show all the characteristics of the Spiritual Community, however, as a social group they show all the multiple ambiguities of religion, culture, and morality. These are the two faces of the church.

One must be careful not to overlook these two faces when regarding the basic character of the Spiritual Community. The Spiritual Community, in respect to that part of the church that is "the body of Christ," is the power that enables the Christian to increase in faith and love. This power is present before the development of one's faith and love, although it does not totally overcome the sinfulness of the individual or institution, such as a church.

Tillich warns us that the Spiritual Community is subject to much misinterpretation. The Spiritual Community must not be interpreted to include an assembly of so-called spiritual beings, angelic hierarchies, saints, and the "saved"—an elect group. This is supernaturalism. It is not in keeping with the reality of the power of the Spiritual Community working within the lives of all those searching for some form of ultimacy.

The paradox of the church—According to Tillich, the paradox of the church is that it is a part of the Spiritual Community, and, at the same time, it is immersed in the same sinfulness characteristic of all other institutions made up of people. One particular problem associated with this is that the church is most often evaluated and judged by society only on its institutional side, with little regard for its spiritual side. It should, instead, be judged on both. The church has two faces, the institutional and spiritual, and care should be taken to include both of them in any judgement. The church's spiritual side contains a mostly invisible Spiritual Community that is the source of the church's power and is what makes the church the church. On its more visible, sociological or institutional side, the church is subject to the same pressures and problems that decide the life of all social institutions.

The church as an institution finds itself struggling to maintain its existence. It has its leadership and power struggles, its problems with communications and commitment, its mortgage, and its internal dissenters. These struggles have resulted in a secular history not unlike many other secular institutions. According to Tillich, however, the churches as institutions are often valued for their important and positive impact as social agencies dedicated to the enhancement of a good life. Churches throughout the world are leaders in humanitarian work. At the same time, critics view churches as instruments of the "status quo" providing support to elitist groups' domination of a world of poverty.

Whatever one's viewpoint, basing the judgement of the churches entirely on their sociological functions and influence is utterly inadequate. A church that is nothing more than a socially useful group can be replaced by other groups not claiming to be churches. It is essential that the spiritual aspect not be overlooked or diminished by the reality of the church's social position. It is the spiritual aspect that points to the presence of the Spiritual Community. It is the power that "drives" the church forward toward the New Being seen in Jesus as the Christ.

Characteristics of the Spiritual Community—There are three special characteristics of the Spiritual Community that Tillich identifies: it is holy, it has unity, and it is universal.

The Spiritual Community is holy for those Spiritual Communities (i.e., the church), that are founded on the New Being, as seen in the life of Jesus the Christ. Tillich tells us that for this reason and this reason alone they are holy. Their holiness is not dependent on the holiness of the church's institutions, doctrines, rituals, devotional activities, or ethical principles, as these are subject to the many problems found within religion as it subjects itself to the sinfulness found within all human institutions. According to Tillich, this characteristic is not true for that part of the latent Spiritual Community found outside of the church.

The second characteristic of the Spiritual Community, unity, also expresses the paradoxical nature of the churches. The unity of the churches derives from their mutual dependence on the Spiritual Community as a source of power. This unity is real in each of them "in spite of" their physical and doctrinal separation. Separation is unavoidable because of the ambiguities of religion, but it does not contradict the unity inherent in their common foundation, the Spiritual Community, which is centered on Jesus the Christ.

The Spiritual Community fights against having a divided church. Its influence can be found in the many attempts to draw the churches together. The most conspicuous example of this is the World Council of Churches. It heals divisions within the church that have become historically obsolete and provide co-operation in social action as well as liturgical practice between churches. According to Tillich, however, no movement can entirely erase the diversity that exists among churches, nor should it. There will always be problems and ambiguities because of the church's sociological existence; importantly so, as the church continues its prophetic criticism (much as the Old Testament Prophets did) and reforms its internal practices at the same time. As the church, it will stimulate new and exciting differences.

The third characteristic of the Spiritual Community is its universality. The Spiritual Community is universal from two standpoints: intensively, in its desire to play a part in all functions of life, and extensively, in the sense of providing a foundation for all nations, social groups, races, tribes, and cultures.

Intensively, the church has historically played a part in all functions of life. Nothing is excluded from the life of the church and its members. Churches are involved politically, socially, culturally, and as land owners, scholars, and educators. No area of life is divorced from the church's activities. This is a particularly strong tradition within the Roman Catholic church of which it can be justifiably proud, according to Tillich. The danger of universality, however, was seen when the world's inherent problems of power, corruption, distortion, and the like, became a major part of the church. This resulted in a revolt, which started the Protestant Reformation of the 16th century.

Extensively, the church is universal, serving as the foundation of nations, social groups, races, tribes and cultures. The New Testament speaks of this through the Apostle Paul, who, through the power of the New Being in Jesus the Christ, unified his own Jewish, Greek, and Roman background. In more recent years the World Council of Churches has functioned as the Church universal, although only partially so, as it does not represent all church bodies.

Churches as a community of faith—When we speak of the faith of the churches or of a particular church, Tillich tells us that there are three considerations of particular consequence:

1. During the time of the early church people joined the church as a part of the community of faith. Their joining was based on a deliberate decision which frequently involved some personal risk due to the persecution of the church at that time. Those that joined were of unquestionable faith. Later in the history of the

church, many people joined, for reasons of faith, but also because of a need for belonging and security. Today, most people, including infants, join rather automatically, following the lead of their parents or as a part of the local culture—the thing to do—not necessarily as an act of faith. In the last two instances an act of faith can not be assumed.

2. The second consideration involves the history of various religious creeds that developed in the early church. According to Tillich, the history of the creeds:

...is a typically ambiguous mixture between Spiritual creativity and the social forces which determine history. The social forces here under consideration are ignorance, fanaticism, hierarchical arrogance, and political intrigue. If the churches require that all their faithful members accept the formulas which came into existence in this way, they impose on them a burden which no one who is aware of the situation can honestly carry....[19]

3. The third consideration involves the question: What does "community of faith" mean if the community, as well as individual members, is disrupted by criticism and doubt from a secular world? Today, perhaps unequaled in history, there is a skeptical or indifferent attitude toward creedal statements among members of the church as well as those outside the church. When society, generally, raises questions and doubts about its faith, it raises, simultaneously, serious questions about the churches being truly a community of faith. These questions are justified, according to Tillich. Though the questions are justified, there is

---

[19.] Tillich, III, p. 174

one irrefutable fact, according to Tillich, that must not be overlooked. It is that Jesus is the Christ, the bringer of the New Being! Given this answer, the church can then be called a community of those who believe that Jesus is the Christ and, therefore, a community of faith. This is what the name Christian means.

Tillich reminds us that many formal members of the church belong entirely for social or political reasons, denying consciously or unconsciously that Jesus is the Christ. Their continued presence in the church can be countenanced, however, as the church is dependent on the divine Spirit rather than on individual decisions by members. Tillich considers this as an ambiguity within the community of faith as it exists within a church.

In a different sense, there are many members of the church with serious doubts whether Jesus is the Christ, who are ambivalent about continuing their membership in the church and the community of faith. They wish to continue their membership, yet feel that they should quit. Many are on the verge of separating themselves from the church because of their doubts about Jesus. Tillich suggests to those in this situation that the important aspect to be considered is the desire (conscious or unconscious) to participate in the life of the church. They should be assured that they fully belong. This is in spite of their doubts about certain of the church's beliefs and doctrinal statements.

Doctrinal statements, creeds, or basic beliefs, are present in all churches to some extent. The approach to them varies considerably, however. On the one hand, as in Roman Catholicism, creedal decisions and statements are considered entirely valid, deviation in belief from them is a heretical separation from the Spiritual Church (the community of faith). In mainline Protestantism, creedal statements are formed and defended, although it is recognized that all doctrines and creedal statements are subject to the imperfections of an ambiguous religion.

Being labeled heretics is not generally the lot of members who question them.

Although Tillich, generally, is troubled by doctrinal statements and creeds, he concludes that the church needs to formulate its own basic creedal foundation and defend it from attacks. To do other than this is to open the possibility of the church's compromise with those in the "church" who may wish to eliminate its foundation in Jesus as the Christ. In preparing a creedal statement the church must protect itself against a doctrine that is destructively exclusive and not subject to modification.

Churches as a community of love—Churches are a community of love as well as a community of faith, and, as such, are subject to all the distortions and conflicts that are a part of churches as institutions. It is the Spiritual Community that provides the church's power through the New Being in Jesus the Christ.

Tillich tells us that as a community of love the church actualizes the Spiritual Community. It makes agape (spiritual) love concrete in cementing relationships between people. In essence, every member of the church is to become the "Good Samaritan." (Lk 10:25-37) The Apostle Paul reminds us in Romans 13:9, of Jesus' command that "You shall love your neighbor as yourself." This he tells us summarizes all other laws. Being a "neighbor" expresses itself in mutual acceptance of all people in spite of differences politically, socially, economically, educationally, nationally, racially, or sexually. Like everything else in the church, however, the community of love that is manifested through the Spiritual Community is ambiguous and imperfect.

According to Tillich, it is important that the churches attack and transform those forms of inequality (political, social, and economic) which make an actual community of love impossible. This includes all forms of suppression and exploitation that destroy the potentialities for humanity in the individual and justice in the group. This is true externally as well as internally within the church itself. The church must lead the way.

In addition to attacking forms of inequality, the church must minister to those who are victims of distortions in society. The material welfare of these victims must be maintained at a level that sustains their potentialities as humans. This is called charity. It is as necessary as it is ambiguous. Charity is a natural extension of the service of love within the church. This is so, although it can serve as a "prop" for "shoring up" and maintaining those institutions that created the victims of injustice. Both issues, attacking inequality and administering charity must be addressed simultaneously.

According to Tillich, the relationship of a particular church, as a community of love, to other communities outside it, is full of problems. The first problem involves what to do concerning those who may attend the church but who are not Christian. The fact of their attending church makes them a part of the latent Spiritual Community and therefore potential future members. Although conversion is necessary to become a member, Tillich considers it to be entirely appropriate to welcome them as fully accepted guests, visitors, or friends. They remain in the latency of the Spiritual Community of the church but as a Jew, Muslim, humanist, and so forth. What is significant is their desire to participate in a group whose foundation is the acceptance of Jesus as the Christ, though they may not personally believe in Jesus the Christ. This should open the door to the community of love called the church.

There is a certain anxiety in some churches with the attendance of members of the latent Christian Community. These churches fear possible distortions of their creeds and doctrines and, as a result, the creeds and doctrines often become increasingly fixed and unchangeable. According to Tillich, this may become a form of fanaticism in which the church insists on its precise doctrinal "rightness." Fanaticism such as this is a result of inner insecurity, feelings of persecution, suspicion, and sometimes hate. When taken to the extreme, these anxieties may produce such events as the witch and heresy trials of the past. It is a genuine fear of the demonic, and, according to Tillich, cannot be overcome by some ideal of tolerance, or attempts to characterize the differences as unimportant. It can be overcome only by the divine Spirit whose love affirms, judges, and reunites people through the New Being in Jesus the Christ.

Problems within the functions of the church—There are many problems within the church which can be overcome through the church's Spiritual Community. Tillich discusses some of them as follows:

1. *Tradition vs reformation*—One of the most important problems is the contrast between tradition and reformation. Tradition is the extension of the church's culture as it has been modified through the years by the active participation of the divine Spirit and New Being. This must be preserved at all cost. On the other hand, reformation is constantly fighting against the problems inherent within religion, also through the power of the divine Spirit and New Being.

The possibility of reformation, through the power of the divine Spirit, is always present within the church. This is an important function of the church, needed to overcome the suppression of freedom by a tradition or dogma within some churches that is often given absolute authority. The suppression of freedom within a church results from the church's anxieties about any change over that which has been declared holy in the past. Guardians of an absolute tradition, according to Tillich, too often suppress the desire for reform, coercing the consciences of those who know better but do not have the courage to push for change.

The two principles, tradition and reformation, however, are unitable within the Spiritual Community, remaining in tension but not in conflict. This is so when the love within the Spiritual Community has sufficient power to minimize conflict.

2. *The "absolute truth" vs "adaption to new realities"*—In the early church some groups demanded the subjection of Christian churches to the Jewish law, the "absolute truth." Most of the groups, however, demanded adapting or meshing the Jewish law with that found in Greek and Hellenistic philosophy. This was essential to the success of the early missionary efforts but in the process of adaptation the content of the Christian message was continuously subject to abuse. This danger was so real that much of the early efforts of the church were involved in its resolution. Without some adaptation in a constantly changing world, however, there are no means to grow and to learn new understandable, and meaningful truths. On the other hand, if adaptations become an unlimited accommodation to all views, the truth of the New Being's message is lost or distorted.

3. *Change*—The church as it actualizes the Spiritual within it must do so through the power of the divine Spirit. Actualizing the Spirit is what makes it a church, separate from a political party, school, or philosophical movement.

The church shows its greatness when the divine Spirit helps it change by moving beyond its norm to ever greater heights, consistent with its foundation in Jesus the Christ. At the same time, there is the possibility of too much change, too fast and too far. If the church falls off the "cutting edge", if all rules that provide the basic integrity of the church as a church are dropped, very little of value will be left. This principle is true not only in the church, but in such areas as personal and social ethics, politics, and education. If change becomes dominant, it can become so overwhelmingly powerful that all structure is thrown "to the wind," violating the basic integrity of the church as an institution. At the other end of the pole, rigidity becomes increasingly meaningless—eventually becoming empty formalism.

Where the divine Spirit is strong in the church the two principles "change" and the "status quo" are in harmony or unity.

4. *Missions*—Mission is as old as when Jesus sent his disciples out to various villages in Israel to "...preach that all should repent..." Mk 6:6b-13. After two thousand years of mission, however, most human beings are still non-Christian, though there are few places on earth that are not at least influenced by Christian culture. In spite of the fragmentary and often ambiguous effects of mission, it continues to be an important primary function of the church.

To Tillich, the purpose of missions is "the actualization of the Spiritual Community within churches all over the world," next door to the "furthest corners of the earth." Tillich's purpose of missions contrasts somewhat with those held by some of the more pietistic denominations whose purpose is to simply save individuals from eternal condemnation. In contrast, Tillich emphasizes a Kingdom of God on earth rather than a salvation or kingdom "to come" somewhere in the "heavens."

One of the ambiguities of religion so often brought up by religious detractors, is the attempt of a religion to impose its cultural forms upon another culture in the name of the New Being in Christ. According to Tillich, it is most difficult for any church to separate the Christian message from the particular culture within which it is being preached. In a sense it is impossible, as the Christian message is not an abstract message. Religion is a part of culture and morality. This ambiguity of missions is overcome when the divine Spirit is sufficiently strong in the missionary effort. Tillich reminds us that this has frequently not been true.

5. *Religious education*—Religious education is one of the major issues confronting the church today. Tillich does not try to diagnosis it by separating it into its parts, suggesting that one part is more effective than another. He does not believe that this is the appropriate realm of the systematic theologian.

Tillich suggests that the religious goals of many churches are not reached because of the manner in which religious education is often taught. In order to be meaningful, the program must include the participation of the students involved. Without participation, understanding is impossible, without understanding, participation is mechanical and perceived as compulsory. A religious educational program, improperly conducted, may alienate rather than educate.

6. *Evangelism*—The church's evangelistic function is directed toward the non-Christian in the world. Although overlapping, there are two general ways to approach the task: (1) by presenting rational proof of the tenets of Christianity, and (2) by evangelistic preaching.

Tillich believes that the best proof of Christianity lies in the behavior of Christians themselves. He acknowledges, however, that rational "proof" is also needed to break through the "intellectual walls" of skepticism, as many people, both inside and outside the church, protect themselves against the power of the divine Spirit. These walls are constantly being built, tending to separate skeptics from the church. Consequently, rational "proof" is needed to appeal to those who are skeptical of Christianity for whatever the reason.

Evangelistic preaching is charismatic, and is dependent upon the emergence of preachers who are able to reach others through the power of the divine Spirit; this type of appeal is generally not present in ordinary preaching. Evangelistic preaching, when preached through the power of the divine Spirit, can transform the listener into a Spiritual awareness and direction not otherwise obtained through the more normal channels of the church. According to Tillich, however, there is a danger in this kind of preaching. If there is not a strong presence of the divine Spirit, visible through faith and love, the results of the preaching produce mere excitement or emotion. This is not a part of the Spiritual Community, though such traditional elements as conversion, repentance, faith, and sanctity, appear to be a part of the process. Too often the "conversion" is only of the moment.

7. *Aesthetics*—Aesthetics, as a special function of the church, uses religious art, poetry, and music to transcend the church's normal life. A

major problem associated with aesthetic expression, according to Tillich, is that it sometimes does not fully and accurately represent what the church professes as its doctrine. The artists involved demand that they be permitted to use the styles to which their artistic conscience drives them. Many artists feel that the old stylistic forms of art do not talk to life as it actually exists. Though some newer forms of art try to do this, they have had only limited success, according to Tillich.

The history of Protestantism reveals great progress over the medieval churches in religious music and hymnical poetry. The Protestant church has, however, fallen very short in the area of visual arts, according to Tillich. This includes religious dance and play, both of which (for various reasons, including fear of idolatry) were condemned by elements in early Protestantism and evangelical radicalism.

8. *Theology*—Theology, the study of God and the relations between God and the universe, interprets the church's symbols based on a criterion of rationality. In this manner, church doctrine and dogma are constantly subject to theological examination. A major problem, according to Tillich, however, is the conflict between what the church accepts as sacred and that which is new as revealed through theological study. Theology continues to probe beyond that contained within the holy scriptures and the church's dogma and doctrine. It is looking for new relevancies regarding the relationship between God and the universe.

9. *The community*—The principle of *justice* within a community is violated whenever a church, or other institution, commits or permits injustice in the name of holiness. Historically, in many religions the king or high priest could suspend principles of justice in respect to their own behavior, and frequently did so. The wrath of the Old Testament prophets was directed against this practice. Within Christian civilization this usually does not happen in exactly the same manner, but it is nevertheless quite real.

In every religion (through their formal hierarchies, or informally through "assumed" degrees of importance among the membership) there is a dependence or close interrelationship—socially and economically—between the church leadership and the leadership of the larger society. In essence they "swim in the same pond." This is one important reason the church so often supports those "in power" within a society, even when the power is exercised unjustly. Examples of support include the alliance of the church's hierarchies with feudal hierarchies during the Middle Ages; and today there is a dependence on the economically and socially influential people in the churches.

Inclusiveness is another problem within the church's function of community. If the church claims to be all-inclusive socially and racially, there is no problem. According to Tillich, however, the church often suffers qualitatively as a result of its intended inclusiveness as it tries to "accommodate" to all the differences within the congregation. Often times this results in the church's unwillingness to make needed changes for fear of alienating portions of its membership.

Regarding *equality*, the church acknowledges the equality of everyone before God within their community as well as without.

> *...show no partiality as you hold the faith of our Lord of glory...and you pay attention to the one who wears fine clothing and say, "Have a seat here, please," while you say to the poor person, "Stand there,"...have you not made distinctions among yourselves, and become judges with evil thoughts...*
> (Jas. 2:1-4)

In practice, however, many churches have established a principle of inequality between the socially acknowledged righteous and the socially condemned sinners. According to Tillich, this is one of the most conspicuous and most anti-Christian denials of what Christ stands for. Some of the worst examples of this neglect is the treatment of "public sinners" by the church, not only in the Middle Ages but today as well. The churches have rarely followed the attitude of Jesus toward the "publicans and the whores." Tillich predicts, that if the churches do not tell of the need for equality in their call to conversion, they will become obsolete. The divine Spirit will then do its work through seemingly atheistic and anti-Christian movements, working toward the equality of all people in the "sight of God."

Leadership is another problem in community. The history of tyranny embraces the largest part of history including that of religion. The continuous attack on religious tyranny by the prophets and apostles did not injure Judaism or the church. It saved it. And so it must today.

Law is related to leadership. Nothing in human history exists for long without laws. Laws "spell out the rules" by which a community lives. One must remember, however, that laws are not a creation of the divine Spirit, though the divine Spirit does guide churches toward a Spiritual use of some laws relating to the needs of society. However, there is great potential for misuse of law. The church is in a constant fight against the ambiguities of power and prestige found in the manipulative use of law.

There is a great deal of resentment in the minds of many people, according to Tillich, toward the so-called "organized church," a legal institution. Unfortunately the resentment carries over into religion itself, not just the "organized church." Tillich tells us that resentment should be directed at the church, but not at religion, as it is the church with its doctrines and beliefs codified into church law that is most subject to criticism.

One must remember that a church is organized in pursuit of symbols and beliefs, and, as such, must have some legal form if it is going to exist as an organized body. Some groups have historically tried to exist without legal form by breaking away from their parent bodies; anarchy was the result. In overcoming the anarchy, the frequent result was new legal forms more oppressive than those previously used. Sometimes, the hostility to "organized religion (church)" becomes so intense that the "community" aspects of religion, an important part of most churches, are renounced, and an attempt made to eliminate the communal aspect from the church. This is opposed by Tillich, as one is dependent upon community for development toward one's ultimate potentiality. One must be continuously nourished by life in the community of faith and love.

10. *Personal and Spiritual growth*—Asceticism and its relationship to personal and spiritual growth is of great concern to Tillich. Some people believe that asceticism is necessary to reach the ultimate in one's growth. Asceticism—historically interchangeable with saintliness by the church—is perceived as providing the channel through which one's divine inner being shows through. One literally resigns from the material world. Those who are able or willing to do this, are considered capable of reaching a level of spirituality higher in the divine-human hierarchy, than those who live in the materially conditioned world.

Tillich rejects this idea. He suggests that asceticism or saintliness such as this, involves the denial of many human potentialities which stops one from focusing on progressing toward full humanity. It denies the doctrine of creation in which the Creator God, "…saw all that God had made, and indeed it was very good…" (Gen 1:31)

Self-discipline is another form of asceticism. The Apostle Paul and John Calvin (a leader in the Protestant Reformation) are examples of those practicing an asceticism of self-discipline. It is based on a strong moral conviction rather than on the simple rejection of the "world." In this form of asceticism, there is a presumption that all of life is immersed in a "fallen state of reality." All of life's temptations must be resisted.

This leads to Puritan repression. The radical restriction of sex and the restraints from many other potentialities of created goodness produced a type of asceticism akin to that practiced by the "saints." This, at times, identified areas of denial that sometimes became rather petty and ludicrous. According to Tillich, churches, today, have generally gotten over this extreme and distorted asceticism practiced in the past. It threatens one's possibility of developing toward one's full humanity.

According to Tillich, asceticism does provide one "plus" to full spiritual and human development. This is a self-discipline that, through the power of the divine Spirit, overcomes one's "exaggerated self-induced importance," providing a humility essential to successful human relationships.

If one chooses a direction in life that is not ascetic, many forces, often in conflict, come to bear on the person, such as parents, teachers, one's career choice, advertisements on T-V and many other influences. In addition, peer pressures and how society rewards success, powerfully influence the direction taken in one's life. The answer that "cuts" through all these influences, according to Tillich, is the power and love available from the divine Spirit. This is not an easy experience, as the divine Spirit helps one to counterbalance all the outside influences present in society.

11. *The church in the world*—The church is constantly working with other institutions in society, influencing them, and in turn being influenced by them. There are three ways that this happens: by working with other groups in society, through speaking out against injustice, and through political means.

Working/relating with other groups (priestly function)—Through its membership, the church has a continuous influence on all groups within society. This is sometimes called the "priestly" function. Many critics of the church often overlook this influence as they criticize what they consider the church's "lack of significance" in today's world. The question needs to be asked, however: What would the world be like in the absence of the church? In spite of the many difficulties the church has had, and continues to have, there has been significant impact on the social fabric of nations through the church's priestly function. Moreover, the influence is mutual, as the church assimilates changing cultural norms into its make up.

Speaking out against injustice (prophetic function)—This is often called the "prophetic" role of the church as it was exercised down through the centuries. It began with the church's criticism and transformation of early imperial Roman society and its paganism. Although its "prophetic" role might seem limited, the church's voice cannot be ignored and some form of action or reaction is certain. This itself is a sign of success.

According to Tillich, churches should encourage prophetic criticism of the negativities in society. They should never forget, however, that the relation is mutual, and society needs to criticize the church when it fails to live up to its Christian mission. Much of the initial criticism of the church by society occurred in the nineteenth and twentieth century through the emergence of scientific inquiry and advances in technology. Sometimes it produced almost unbridgeable differences between the church and large groups in society. Beyond this, according to Tillich, it provided insights to the church that resulted in the church's revision of how justice and humanity are interpreted.

The political—One task of church leaders at all levels, according to Tillich, is to influence the leaders of other social groups in a way that protects the right of the church's priestly and prophetic function. They must consistently do this within the command of love which excludes the use of military force, misleading and inflammatory propaganda, the arousal of religious fanaticism, and similar behaviors.

As the church finds a commonality between other institutions and itself, there is the danger that it will become like the other institutions. This commonality places the church in danger of losing its very essence. Its holiness may turn into "absoluteness," and it may fall into a demonic self-righteousness. An important danger here, is the possible use of its power and influence, priestly, prophetic, and political, in support of the institution, i.e., the state, that it has become a part. This is what happened when the church became a part of the Roman Empire during the reign of Emperor Constantine and later became a part of the Feudalism of the Middle Ages. A nationalistic ideology asserting that the needs of a particular state were paramount over all other needs of society, seriously weakened the church's prophetic function. Churches, too often, became a tool of the state, participating in the state's national sacraments and rites that reinforced the "status quo" of the national leadership. The church became impotent due to its domination by the state, finally culminating with the Protestant Reformation and the Renaissance.

Unfortunately, according to Tillich, this may have separated the church so far from other institutions, that the church lost much of its priestly and prophetic power in the name of the separation of church and state.

The individual, the church, and the divine Spirit—Churches may be looked at as organizations in two separate ways: those that emphasize the individual member over the institutional church and those that emphasize the institutional church over the individual member.

In the first type, *the individual over the church*, a decision is made by individuals to come together and, working together with the divine Spirit, begin a church. It is a voluntary effort on the part of individuals.

This situation changes, however, starting with the second generation. At this point, individuals are drawn to an already existing church by the atmosphere of family and friends; what was a voluntary decision now becomes an expectation of the church. At this point the church is predominant over the individual.

In this latter case, the individual enters a church that is already existing. One enters the church consciously or unconsciously (as an infant), as there is no point in a person's life that can be identified as the precise time of spiritual maturity. This is the theological justification, according to Tillich, for infant baptism.

Regarding the semi-sacramental act of "confirmation"—practiced by many churches at about the fourteenth year—Tillich suggests that it may result in congregational pressure forcing youngsters to make a personal decision concerning their relationship to God and the church rather than making the decision based on faith. When this is the case, according to

Tillich, the reactions of children may reflect the psychologically unhealthy and theologically unjustifiable character of this act. God does not intend that children be pressured into premature decisions.

The really important concern in all of this is how an individual can become a member of the Spiritual Community through participation in a church. According to Tillich, there is no specific point in a person's life in which the beginning of this type of participation can be identified. This is true whether the person was "born in the church" or "discovers" the church later in life. In neither instance, can one determine the exact moment that one became a member of the Spiritual Community, unlike knowing the exact moment when formally joining a church.

Tillich recognizes that this seems to contradict the concept of conversion that plays such a predominant role in both Testaments, in the history of the church, and in the life of many Christians throughout the world (conversion standing for that point in time when a person enters the Spiritual Community). But conversion, according to Tillich, is most often not a momentary event; often it is preceded by an unconscious process that has been going on for a long time before it breaks into consciousness. This may give an impression of suddenness but it is not sudden and has occurred, generally, over many years.

True conversion, to Tillich, demands a change in direction for one's life, from a life dominated by estrangement, to a life affirmed by a New Being in Jesus the Christ. This is known as *repentance*. Affirmation of the presence of the New Being in one's life is called a *declaration of faith*. True and lasting entry into the Spiritual Community involves great preparation which, without conversion, would be nothing more than an emotional outburst with little permanent consequences.

Conversion usually has the character of transition rather than of "sudden awareness." It is a transition from the inactive or hidden stage of the Spiritual Community to the active and visible stage. This is the real structure of conversion, according to Tillich; it implies that repentance and faith are not, at any single moment in time, completely new.

There is no absolute conversion, only relative conversion—a corner is turned, or a direction bent into a new direction. This way of looking at conversion has a great bearing on the church's evangelistic efforts. According to Tillich, the function of these efforts is not simply that of converting the person who is a "lost soul" (as is traditionally believed), but to gain one's active participation in the Spiritual Community.

When people enter a church, they are subjected to the increasing influence of the divine Spirit. They become a New Being through what is called, theologically, the processes of regeneration, justification by faith not works, and sanctification.

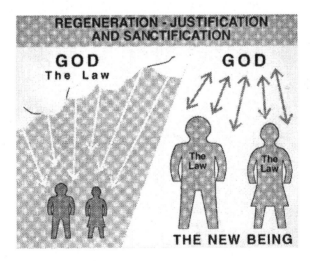

1. *Regeneration*—According to Tillich, regeneration naturally leads to the questions: How does a person have a new birth? Am I really reborn? If I am not, does that mean that I am rejected by God? The last question essentially destroys the message of the Gospels which means the "good news." The good news of the Gospels is that God never rejects

a person even though all people fall far short of God's ideal for them. The "unacceptable" are accepted by God, whose love is freely given through faith, a faith created through the divine Spirit. It can then be asked: If the divine Spirit must grasp me and create faith in me, what can I do to find such faith? According to Tillich, the answer to this question is implied in the question itself. One who is ultimately concerned about one's separation from God, and the possibility of reunion with God, is experiencing the New Being of faith.

2. *"Justification by grace (love), through faith, not works"*— Justification by grace, through faith, not works, is the central doctrine of the Sixteenth Century Protestant Reformation. In essence, it tells us that it is not in the power of an individual to reunite with God; only God is able to reunite with a person. No human claim, religious, intellectual, moral or devotional "work," can do this. The power to reunite comes from God and is a free gift available to all. All one must do is accept God's gift.

The word "justification," within this principle, needs some explanation. According to Tillich, the biblical term justification was used extensively by many early Christians who were used to being "judged" under the Jewish law. Justification to them became the act of being judged by God against the criteria of law. Although the Apostle Paul used the term, he used it in the sense of "acceptance" by God, through God's love, although we are "unacceptable" according to the criteria of law. All we need do is accept the fact of our "acceptance" in spite of our inability to live by every requirement of the law.

How can one know that one is accepted by God? How does one know for certain that one is forgiven? The answer, according to Tillich, lies in the nature of God's unconditional love for a humanity that is accepted by God no matter what; acceptance is not conditioned on specific acts of justice or injustice.

Tillich rejects the possibility that God "draws a line" at half-goodness being acceptable and anything less than half-goodness as not acceptable. This is not consistent with a God of love and justice. God, instead of judging the degree of goodness in an individual, points one toward the divine goodness of love and justice. One is moved by the divine Spirit in this direction, overcoming the need to concentrate on the justice or injustice of specific acts.

According to Tillich, all of this occurs through the crucifiction of Jesus. God, through Jesus the Christ, became a part of our sinful world, overcame it, never yielding even when nailed to a cross. God, having lived within a sinful world and, at the same time, having overcome it through the cross, can understand and accept what is otherwise an unacceptable humanity. The victory of Jesus over sin becomes our victory.

But what about the person of great doubt who may include the rejection of all that is religious? To a person such as this, "God, and accepting the unacceptable," has no meaning. The question of what one can do to overcome this doubt, according to Tillich, cannot be answered satisfactorily. Tillich suggests that it is impossible to reach God entirely by intellectual understanding or moral works. He reminds us that God is the acting agent not ourselves. As Paul tells us in the book of Romans:

> ...*since all have sinned and fall short of the glory of God, they are justified by his grace (love) as a gift, through the redemption which is in Christ Jesus....(Romans 3:23-24)*

If there is an answer for the person of great doubt, it lies in the seriousness of the despair that asks the question. The divine Spirit is found in the ultimate honesty of the doubt and the seriousness of the despair about the possibility of an ultimate meaning of life.

3. *Sanctification*—Two movements began within the Protestant Reformation, one was started by Martin Luther and the other by John Calvin. Luther and Calvin agreed about two functions of the Old Testament law: (1) that of directing the life of an individual, by either

preventing or punishing law breaking, and (2) that of showing a person what one essentially is and what one ought-to-be.

Calvin, however, spoke of a third function as well, that of sanctification which is a theological concept meaning "the process through which one actually transforms one's life" through the presence of the New Being. In sanctification, a perfectionist ideal was visualized producing a movement that equated salvation with moral perfection in individual persons. Luther, in contrast, saw sanctification as a process of ecstasy followed by anxiety in something of an up-and-down process.

Calvinism, with its perfectionist approach, produced a type of Protestant ethic in which progressive sanctification was the aim of life. It had a tremendous effect in shaping powerful, self-disciplined individuals. An "inner-worldly asceticism" appeared which placed high value on work, self-control, and repression of sexual vitality. Through the years Calvinism has been adopted by various Evangelical churches who, with their ideal of total perfection, strengthened the perfectionist elements of Calvinism.

Lutherism, in contrast, envisions a person being alternatively seized by God's love, and then released into sin and estrangement. Moments of ecstasy and joy, also despair, would be experienced. Sanctification could not be interpreted in terms of a line moving upward toward perfection, as in Calvinism. Within Lutherism, however, there was a general lack of discipline, according to Tillich, which resulted in progressive sanctification being taken less seriously than in Calvinism and Evangelic traditions.

Luther placed a greater emphasis on the contradictory character of the Christian life, than did Calvin. His approach to sanctification provided for little discipline and led to some degree of moral disintegration and a "practical" religion. This was unfortunate, according to Tillich, but it did prepare the way for the second period of Romanticism, particularly as experienced in Europe. The people of the eighteenth and nineteenth century made great strides in the fine arts and literature, emphasizing passion over reason, imagination and inspiration over logic. This period could not have sprung from a Calvinistic-Evangelistic movement with its emphasis on discipline.

The ideal goal of sanctification is sainthood (perfection). The term saint, though, has had various meanings, initially meaning membership in a church congregation. Obviously, all the members of a congregation, at any period of the church's history, were not saints as we commonly understand the meaning of saint today. Nevertheless, the New Testament, in particular, those parts attributed to the Apostle Paul, refers to saints as a common term for the members of a church, or as the equivalent to being a Christian.

The meaning of "saint" changed when the early church began to attribute a special saintliness to the ascetics and the martyrs. The ordinary members of the church ceased to be saints. The idea behind the new "saints" was that those so designated by the church have some form of power over nature and humanity. They were not necessarily morally superior, they simply had more power. A saint, in essence, was one who has performed some miracles. This idea of sainthood continues within the Roman Catholic church today.

Protestantism rejects the concept of saint altogether. According to Tillich, there are three primary reasons for this. First, the distinction made between those designated saints and all other Christians, implies that it is possible to reach a state of perfection. This contradicts the Protestant emphasis on the sinfulness of all persons and the need for justification (or acceptance) by God through the death of Jesus on the cross. Secondly, according to Protestantism, the saints became objects of cults or sects within the church, e.g., the Franciscan order, named after St. Francis. Protestantism wishes to protect itself against idolatry as they perceive this to be. Finally, Protestantism does not recognize saints due to the emphasis of sainthood on an ascetic life and the seeming denial of the goodness of God's creation.

Although Protestantism does not recognize saints, it does recognize representatives of the Spiritual Community who manifest a strong divine Spirit in their lives. They are no more saints than any other members of the Spiritual Community, however. Within their lives there is the same struggle that confronts all humanity—the struggle between the divine and the demonic.

Some Protestant churches believe that the highest point that can be realized through the process of sanctification is mystical union with God. This idea, easily accepted by pietistic groups, was radically rejected by many others, with mysticism playing only a minor role in most Protestant churches. Although a great deal of mysticism exists in the saint's image of perfection in the Roman Catholic church, it is rejected by most of Protestantism, as contradicting the aim of sanctification, which is the development of a personal day-to-day relationship with God through faith in Jesus the Christ.

Tillich tells us that mystical experiences should not be excluded from the process of sanctification, as has so often been done by the Protestant church. Every religious experience includes some form of mysticism. The fact that Protestantism did not understand its relation to mysticism has resulted in the rejection of Christianity by many Eastern religions— Zen Buddhism being an example.

Tillich's view of sanctification is much broader than either Calvin's or Luther's. It is based on four principles or processes: increasing awareness, increasing spiritual freedom, increasing relatedness, and increasing transcendence. These four principles, together, are the essence of the Christian life as far as Tillich is concerned.

The first principle, *increasing awareness*, is related to contemporary depth psychology (the study of the unconscious) although it is as old as religion and is addressed throughout the New Testament. It is the process within which one becomes increasingly aware of that which is divine in one's life, as well as the "demonic" forces, internal and external, that "drag one under." Awareness does not make a person "wise." Instead of this, it leads one toward a life of understanding, which provides the ability to value or affirm all that is good in spite of the many ambiguities within one's life. Such awareness includes a sensitivity toward the need for a continuous personal growth experience, as well as an appreciation for the needs and aspirations of others. Awareness such as this occurs under the impact of the divine Spirit.

The second principle, *increasing spiritual freedom*, is, first of all, freedom from the law and the guilt and anxiety produced by trying to live under its heavy demand. This is one of the major tenets of the Apostle Paul in Galatians 3:23; 4:1-7; 5:1-3; and Romans 8:2, 21. The more one is immersed in the love of God (which is the spirit of the law), the more one is free from servitude (brought on by the letter of the law). Living within the spirit of God's love, although imperfectly, frees one from the exact commandments of law. This is not to say that specific laws that contain the experience and the wisdom of the past are unimportant, they are important; they are, however, both helpful and oppressive, as they cannot meet the concrete, ever new, unique situation. The mature freedom to create new laws or to apply the old ones differently is an aim during sanctification. The principle of increasing freedom implies a courage to risk a wrong decision in this regard. The danger that such freedom may turn out to be willfulness is overcome whenever the reuniting power of the divine Spirit is effective.

The third principle, *increasing relatedness*, is the overcoming of one's self-seclusion and the reaching out in understanding to another. Innumerable barriers exist in overcoming these problems such as one's introversion and sometimes hostility toward others, in particular a hostility directed toward people outside of one's immediate family or those who think or look a bit differently.

The New Being, through the reuniting power of God's love, drives one toward a mature relatedness. Only God's love can overcome the hostility and self-centeredness that frequently exists in one's relationships with others. Tillich does not mean to deny that relationships do not exist outside the power of God's uniting love; he does suggest that these are, at best, transitory and ambiguous, combining elements of love and estrangement. Human relationships, exclusively on their own, cannot conquer loneliness, self-seclusion, self-centeredness, and hostility. A symptom of spiritual maturity is the power to sustain solitude, in contrast to being lonely. It is not becoming an extrovert. The process of sanctification provides one the ability to grow toward God. Growth toward God, provides one the ability and desire to relate to others through God's love.

The fourth principle, *increasing transcendence*, includes within it awareness, freedom, and relatedness. They cannot be separated out. Any form of sanctification is impossible without a continuous movement of oneself in the direction of God. One must take part in God's holiness.

Taking part in God's holiness is usually thought of as one's devotional life. However, if devotional life is perceived exclusively as that part of life involved in prayer—as a specific act—then it is very limiting. Tillich suggests that one's devotional life may include all of one's life within which there is an attitude of devotion toward God. This may include one's holy life as well as secular life.

He does not make a distinction between formalized and private devotion. To pray in solitude, or to contemplate without words, are acts of devotion, just as much as participating in the church's devotion. No law requires one to participate in religious services in order to have a devotional life. Tillich strongly suggests, however, that participation in the devotional life of the church enhances one's own devotional life as well as protecting one from the possibility of producing a vacuum in which devotional life disappears.

According to Tillich, one's devotional life is possible in every act in which the presence of the divine Spirit is experienced. This can be in prayer, meditation, in relationships with others, in creative works of art, or simply while working or resting. Sanctification's four principles, collectively, will not lead a Christian directly to perfection, as perfection is not possible. The principles will, however, be evident in all phases of one's Christian life that leads toward God.

The Divine Spirit within Culture

The divine Spirit, religion and culture—Tillich begins this section by suggesting that religion, through the divine Spirit, has the power to overcome all of life's ambiguities no matter what they may be. This is true, even though religion itself has many ambiguities of its own. Of particular importance to Tillich, is the understanding that the divine Spirit not only works within the church but also works within secular institutions, though it is true that the church is an important medium through which the divine Spirit works. One must never overlook the fact that the divine Spirit is present in all individuals and institutions, awakening their social conscience.

This is in at least partial conflict with those who suggest the only way to overcome the many serious ambiguities of culture, which are often destructive, is to strengthen religion. This is just not so, according to Tillich. The mistake made is to believe that the divine Spirit is bound to religion. This serves to limit the freedom of the Spirit by the absolute claim of a religious group.

There is, however, an essential belongingness of religion and culture together as religion is the substance of culture, its depth, that which shapes the future of culture, while culture provides the form or language within which religion exists.

Theonomy and humanism—Theonomy is the state of the culture under the impact of the divine Spirit. Included within a theonomous culture is the aim that all humans will develop toward a loving, transcendent God. It is important to note that the aim or direction comes from within theonomy, it is not externally imposed. In contrast, humanism, which also has lofty goals for the development of people, avoids the question of direction. Humanism does not say what direction human development should go.

According to Tillich, a theonomous culture can be jeopardized by what is called heteronomy, which is a cultural direction based upon laws from outside the culture, either of ecclesiastical or political origin. Theonomy can never be completely defeated by heteronomy, however, any more than it can be completely victorious. Its victory is always partially due to the estranged and sinful condition of humans. Its defeat, however, is always limited because human nature is essentially theonomous.

A theonomous culture can best be understood by looking at its "trappings"—a painted flower, a particular relationship with another person, the development of an improved health system, a particular political document or speech, such as the Gettysburg Address, and so on. None of these creations may be consecrated by a church, but in a larger sense they may be consecrated by the quality of experience they produce.

Tillich suggests that there are several characteristics of a theonomous culture deserving special attention. It must, as an example, communicate an experience of holiness, of something ultimate in being and meaning, in all that it does. Another characteristic is the affirmation of one's right to creative self-expression. There is no theonomy where justice is rejected in the name of God, or where an act of self-determination is prevented by a sacred tradition, or where a new style of creative expression is suppressed in the name of some form of absoluteness that rejects the new.

The divine Spirit and theonomy—Every past, present, and future event that occurs in the world is subject to disagreement. This is true in the sense that every person perceives the event differently, particularly regarding its effect on the whole range of possible outcomes. Therefore, the only truth one can know for sure is, at best, incomplete, regarding its relationship to the whole. According to Tillich, however, where the Spirit is present this problem is alleviated, and the distortions of understanding are overcome.

The effect of the divine Spirit on theonomous relationships may also be felt in the pursuit of technological advancement. Without the power of the divine Spirit, the "means and ends" involved in technical progress become highly complicated. According to Tillich, we too often fail to ask "What is the result of technical progress?" This is seldom determined and even when it seemingly is, the result, when reached, becomes the means to additional advancement, and so on, ad infinitum. The results are subject to no direction; they are rudderless. If it were a theonomous relationship, however, there would be a process in which all "means" would be subject to a test of whether their "end" results fit into an ultimate end. If not, the culture itself would limit the freedom to go beyond this end.

Unfortunately, a theonomous culture under the influence of the divine Spirit, which attempts to limit technical advancement, is subject to corruption by competitive or mercenary interests, according to Tillich. Emptiness of the spirit

> ...is fostered by the business and advertisement supported drives toward the production of what is called the "gadget." The gadget itself is not evil, but gearing a whole economy to it and repressing the question of an ultimate end of all production of technical goods is....[20]

A theonomous culture, propelled by the divine Spirit, can revolutionize humanity's attitudes toward gadgets. It can do this by insisting

---

20. Tillich, III, p. 259.

upon gadgets that lead toward the betterment of society as a whole. According to Tillich, under the influence of the divine Spirit the destructive side of all technical development would be banned.

There are also relationship problems between persons that would be vastly improved within a theonomous culture. How often do we label the "other person" as different from ourselves because of behavior, color of skin, ethnic origin, as well as other differences. The development of one's full humanity can only be realized through reunion with those who are "different." According to Tillich, humanity, as God would have it develop, requires union with the "stranger." We are all a part of humanity. We are all a part of God's creation.

Reunion, outside the power of the divine Spirit, most often involves an effort to make the stranger the same as yourself. The stranger takes the opposite direction—trying to make you the same as he or she. A constant struggle is the result, sometimes one or the other person predominates; either way, however, the one who is dominant tries to influence or control the other. In a theonomous relationship, however, those in conflict rise above their current situation, instead of conflict, they learn from each other, coming together as they approach the ultimate aim in life, God.

To be a community, there must be an exclusiveness. This occurs the moment one defines the community. Inclusive-exclusive relationships can have both good and bad aspects. In the former sense they can foster close, nurturing relationships important to the growth of secure, loving individuals; in the latter case, they can be oppressive by excluding people based entirely on such factors as race, religion, or sex. Under the influence of the divine Spirit a theonomous relationship can evolve in all communities, valuing universal inclusiveness, without losing the identity of the group. When churches, in particular, are transformed from exclusive religious communities, with rigid, dogmatic doctrine, into holy communities, with universal inclusiveness, they have a powerful impact upon all secular communities with which they are in contact.

Another societal problem of community that can be overcome through a theonomous culture involves the area of inequality. Justice, which most people believe is a desirable characteristic of a society, implies equality. However, trying to make that which is naturally unequal, equal, is just as unjust as making that which is naturally equal, unequal. In a theonomous culture, under the influence of the divine Spirit, the ultimate equality of all people in the eyes of God is recognized and cherished within the Spiritual Community. In so far as social institutions are theonomous, the ultimate equality of humans in the eyes of God provides the very fabric of the society or social institution.

One of the most difficult problems within a community is that of leadership and power. The community sometimes takes on the characteristics of a powerful leader, and, when this occurs, tyranny is the result. In the opposite vein, a leaderless, revolutionary anarchy may oppose this tyranny, ultimately taking it over. The result is as bad as the original tyranny. In a theonomous culture, under the influence of the divine Spirit, the rulers subject the direction of their leadership to the will of the group—in essence a democratic institution is formed. The rulers give power to the community; the community accepts power from the rulers. This type of democratic ideal can be present in all societies, even those with aristocratic and monarchial leadership. Beware of democracies, however, that hide behind the "democratic" ideal but, in fact, corrupt or otherwise demonize it. This will not occur to the degree that the community is under the impact of the divine Spirit.

Tillich now addresses several difficult problems associated with the relationship between the establishment of law and its just execution. As an example, legal power, exercised by the leadership in power, is inseparably tied to a justice system created and carried out by the leadership. It is a justice system representing their value system, and at a minimum, sustains their continued roles as leaders. Through the power of the divine Spirit, the law can receive a theonomous quality to the extent that the Spirit is effective. The divine Spirit removes the law's injustices by fighting the narrow interests that support the injustice. This fight, according to Tillich, has sometimes been waged through the voice of the churches and the Spiritual Community and sometimes by prophetic movements within secular society.

Another problem with the legal system is its execution. The execution of law is dependent on the power of those who render judgments and how they represent the best interest of society or simply their own interests. The Old Testament prophets exhorted judges to exercise justice against their own class interests and against their changing moods. There are many problems associated with the execution of the law, in particular, the law's inability to fit any concrete case in a precise manner. New, more specific laws are then passed, and the situation becomes even more confused. The new laws are equally inadequate. The true wisdom of the law lies between the law itself and its application to a concrete situation. This wisdom can be theonomously inspired through the power of the divine Spirit.

The Divine Spirit, Religion and Morality

The divine Spirit: theonomous ethics—Theonomous ethics are ethics in which religious matters are discussed under the influence of the divine Spirit and freely debated without religious dogma dominating or influencing the outcomes. Tillich dismisses the possibility of discussing specific ethics exclusively within a theological context, as a theological discussion is subject to influence by church doctrine or dogma. In other words ethics, within a theological context, are predetermined and are consciously prejudiced.

The divine Spirit: problems of self-integration—In the life of many people the question of the direction to go with one's life is of continuous concern. According to Tillich, people do not know where to go, so they go nowhere, leading a life of no-change, no-growth, of narrow provincialism. On the other hand, there are those who are tempted to go in all directions, try to do so, and end up not really pursuing any direction in depth or intensity. The divine Spirit overcomes these concerns, although only partially, by providing one the internal strength necessary to maintain one's balance. When doing this, the person moves consistently toward the direction of the ultimate, God.

Tillich reminds us that none of us can do all things as it is impossible to do so. Only the sum of all individuals can do this. A person's potentialities remain undeveloped or underdeveloped in every moment of one's life. Some potentialities are simply impossible to develop due to economic, cultural, political, and personal reasons of health, or it's simply a matter of priority or availability of time. Some potentialities of an individual must be sacrificed due to one's personal, human limits.

In contrast to the humanist's idea of one being able to fully develop all of one's potential, those under the guidance of the divine Spirit concentrate on those potentialities that lead toward the ultimate in God. Jesus speaks to this point when he says:

> …*But seek first God's kingdom and God's righteousness, and all these things shall be yours as well…(Matthew 6:33).*

The divine Spirit: problems of the moral law—Humans are constantly subjected to fluctuations between abstract general laws of behavior and the concrete situations one faces each hour of the day. Trying to apply general moral laws to unique and specific situations makes most ethical judgment ambiguous.

Love, in the sense of agape, is the criterion of all ethical judgments, which eliminates the ambiguity. The wisdom of the ages, ethical experiences of the past, revelatory experiences, are often expressed in the moral laws of religion and philosophy. Under the impact of prophetic criticism, they must change their meaning when they no longer help in the concrete situation—if they are obsolete, they are destructive. They were once created by love, but are now in conflict with love. They have become the letter of the law rather than the spirit. Love itself uses wisdom, transcending the wisdom of the past.

With respect to specific moral content, theonomous morality is determined by the love emanating from the divine Spirit. This starts with the wisdom of the past, but is made concrete and adequate by the application of the courage of love to the unique situation, overcoming unjust and inadequate doctrines of the past. A courage such as this runs the risk of being wrong. All ethics, not under the impact of the divine Spirit, produce laws that increase rather than reduce one's estrangement.

The Divine Spirit, Healing, Its Relationship to Life

The divine Spirit and life in general—According to Tillich, the divine Spirit directly influences only the dimension of the spirit. The divine Spirit has no direct impact on the inorganic, the organic, or on self-awareness. When affecting the human spirit, it does not do so in an intoxicating manner, or as a stimulus for psychological excitement, or as a cause that affects some miraculous physical change or direction.

This must be emphasized, according to Tillich, in view of the many instances in the history of religion (including the Bible) in which the Spirit, as divine power, is mistakenly thought to remove a person from one place to another "through the air"; kill a healthy but immoral person by mere words; create an embryo without male participation; or produce a knowledge of foreign languages without the speaker ever studying them. If these stories are taken literally, rather than as symbols of theological truth, they make the divine Spirit a cause, among all other causes in the physical world. In this view the Spirit is a kind of physical matter, and both its Spirituality and divinity are lost.

An additional point made by Tillich is that the divine Spirit, although not having a direct impact on life other than in the dimension of the spirit, has an indirect impact on all of life due to life's multidimensional unity. If all dimensions are actually or potentially present in all other dimensions, then happenings in one dimension have at least an indirect impact on other dimensions. As an example, the impact of the divine Spirit on the creation of a theonomous morality, also has an effect on the psychological well being of humans, their physical well being and the many physiological and chemical processes involved.

The divine Spirit, healing, and salvation—All dimensions of life are involved in healing, including that of the spirit. Salvation is a form of healing, and healing is an element of salvation.

Disease occurs within a human when the body, mind, or spirit fails to change with a changing world or it changes so rapidly that disease is the result. This may result from either internal or external forces or circumstances. Healing forces within organic processes (internally triggered within the body, or externally imposed through such areas as surgery, drugs, or psychotherapy) try to heal the disease. Failure to treat the disease adequately may lead to an early death.

Processes of disintegration that produce diseases are taking place continuously within everyone. At the same time, processes of healing are also occurring through other than natural healing and medical doctor's skills. Spiritual healing, according to Tillich, is one process of primary importance. This should never be overlooked.

In addition to spiritual healing, Tillich addresses the matter of what is commonly called "faith" healing or healing under the influence of the divine Spirit. Tillich suggests that faith healing be called "magic healing." Faith healing movements, as they are generally known, are acts of concentration or forms of autosuggestion. They are produced ordinarily by acts of another person or groups of persons, although not exclusively so. This type of healing appears to have been successful in many instances, but it is in no way, according to Tillich, related to the genuinely religious concept of faith, which is the state of being grasped by the divine Spirit.

He does not call faith healing magic in a negative sense. He defines magic as the impact of one being on another—the propagandist, the teacher, the preacher, the counselor, the doctor, the lover, the friend—all have a magic impact on others in some manner. He suggests that three things must be stated with respect to magic healing: (1) it is not healing by faith but by concentration, (2) it is justified as a part of human encounter, and has both creative and destructive elements, and (3) if it excludes other ways of healing it is predominantly destructive. As his final example of "magic healing," Tillich uses prayers of intercession that are magical concentrations on the desired aim, a return to health, using God for its realization.

Regarding the healing impacts of the divine Spirit, they do not replace all other processes of healing, nor do all other processes of healing replace the process of healing under the impact of the Spirit. Healing is fragmentary in all its forms. Disease is in a continuous struggle with health; disease initiated in one realm may initiate health in another; health in one realm may initiate disease in another realm (for example, a neurotic athlete or a psychotic social activist). All processes of healing, together, no matter where the origin of the disease, are sometimes needed to return to health (if a return is possible). Tillich points out that healing should involve the appropriate use of combinations of healing processes, not relying exclusively on but one process.

No healing, not even that under the impact of the divine spirit, can liberate a person from one's eventual death. Therefore, the question of healing extends beyond the immediate, to the healing involved in salvation and the question of Eternal Life and the Kingdom of God.

Commentary

This chapter of Paul Tillich's *Systematics* may be a bit heavy for some. To relieve the stress, somewhat, the following quotations are offered, hopefully, to broaden one's perspective a bit:

Nature gave people two ends—one to sit on and one to think with. Ever since then people's success or failure has been dependent on the one used the most.

George R. Kirkpatrick

And I said to the man who stood at the gate of the year: "Give me a light, that I may tread safely into the unknown." And he replied: "Go out into the darkness and put your hand into the hand of God. That shall be to you better than light and safer than a known way."

Minnie Louise Haskins

Republics come to an end by luxurious habits; monarchies by poverty.

Montesquieu: De l'Esprit des Lois

When ideas fail, words come in very handy.

Goethe

When you don't have any money, the problem is food. When you have money, it's sex. When you have both, it's health. If everything is simply jake, then you're frightened of death.

J.P. Donleavy

There's no better way of exercising the imagination than the study of the law. No poet ever interpreted nature as freely as a lawyer interprets truth.

Jean Giraudoux
French dramatist

First secure an independent income, then practice virtue.

Greek saying

When work is a pleasure, life is a joy! When work is a duty, life is slavery.

Maxim Gorky

Democracy means government by discussion but it is only effective if you can stop people talking.

Clement Attlee
British statesman

In order to see Christianity, one must forget almost all the Christians.

Henri Frederic

It is a mistake to assume that God is interested only, or even chiefly, in religion.

William Temple
British Archbishop

Die when I may, I want it said of me by those who know me best, that I have always plucked a thistle and planted a flower where I thought a flower would grow.

Abraham Lincoln

I'm not afraid to die. I just don't want to be there when it happens.

Woody Allen

Discussion

1. What is the difference between a Spiritual Community and a church?

2. Discuss the implications for the church in its "failure" to recognize the equality of all people whether inside or outside the church. What does Tillich mean by equality?

3. Presuming that Tillich's description of the "secular" church is accurate, how might it be better understood and presented to the public within a better contextual framework? Is it important to do this?

4. Are creedal and doctrinal statements important to the proper functioning of a church? How much is enough?

5. Are churches inclusive in your experience? Is it possible for a church to include within its "family" those with all imaginable viewpoints ranging from the ultra-conservative to new ageism?" Is there ever a need to be exclusive? How might a church accommodate to such a wide diversity?

6. Do you agree with Tillich's views on asceticism?

7. Is the church redeeming its prophetic function? Should it be taking a more active role regarding correcting the root causes of injustice within society?

8. Explain in your own words "justification by grace, through faith, not works." Does this have a tendency to "water down" the church's prophetic function?

9. Explain what Tillich means by theonomy?

CHAPTER 6

The Trinity

The Trinitarian doctrine—Within Judaic and Christian tradition there is only one God. This is made clear throughout the Old and New Testaments beginning in the book of Exodus "...You shall have no other gods before me..." (Exodus 20:3). Tillich tells us that it is important to reconfirm this tradition as this is the God of Jesus the Christ.

Though Tillich believes strongly in one God, he does not agree with that part of the tradition that portrays the God of the Bible as an all knowing and all powerful God—a God who rules the universe by edict.

Tillich does not believe that God orchestrates all that occurs in the universe, instead he believes in a God who influences the outcomes of the human experience, sharing in its joy and sorrow, rather than one that controls human events and is divorced from human reality.

Although there is only one God in Christianity, Christian Trinitarian doctrine includes within its concept three separate facets of the one God: (1) God the Father/Mother, (2) God the Son/Daughter, and (3) God the divine Spirit. This raises an important question. In spite of the stated tradition of one God is there in fact three Gods? Or is there only one God who is the ultimate of everything that exists and two lesser Gods of diminished divine status?

According to Tillich, this is not so much a problem of numbers as much as a problem of role. What is the relation between God and Jesus the Christ? Some Christians in the early church believed that Jesus was the highest of all humans, but decidedly human. If this belief had prevailed, Jesus would have been in need of salvation as a human. Christianity has rejected this idea, however, as it is contrary to the belief that Jesus was sinless and, as the Christ, overcame the sinfulness of the secular world, rising above it into the holy realm of God.

The question of whether Jesus was God, human, or both, or whether there are three facets of God, distinct from each other, yet representing the same complete truth and love, leaves us with something of a riddle. As far as Tillich is concerned, there has never been a satisfactory answer to this riddle. He suggests that, if there is a difference in function, God the Creator, Jesus the redeemer, and the Holy Spirit active within the spirit of humans, don't we then have 3 gods rather than one?

The Trinitarian Problem—Tillich does not profess to have the "ultimate" solution to the understanding of Trinitarianism. He suggests, however, that respect and acknowledgment be given to the symbol, even though it has become an incomprehensible mystery perhaps never to be fully understood. Trinitarianism has, unfortunately, become the center of dissension and disputes in some churches. The three central symbols God, Jesus and the divine Spirit (Holy Spirit) were originally intended to express the appearance of God to human beings through the life of Jesus, and, in doing so, provide answers to the question of the meaning of existence. The original intent has now been replaced by arguments.

Failing to adequately clarify the mystery of Trinitarianism has another important consequence. It has resulted in a Protestant Christianity that has, to a substantial degree, reduced the "teachings of Jesus" to a source book for moral teaching, rather than as a means to better understand God as God, of the mystery of divinity, of a divine Spirit, and of the character of faith, love, and prayer.

Tillich, for all his concerns about the state of Trinitarian dogma, believes that it can regain its proper place in theological thought. He suggests, however, that to do so will require a new and revised understanding of the divine Life and the divine Spirit, including that of male-female symbolism. To this end, Tillich introduces the concept "ground of being" which points to the mother-quality of giving birth, a quality attributed to God. Unfortunately, a demanding father-image of God has shaped the religious and moral consciousness of the past. It is obvious, however, that God is the power of being in all respects, male and female; so there must be no predominance of the male element in the symbolization of the divine.

As far as Tillich is concerned, the doctrine of the Trinity is not closed. We must not totally discard or accept the traditional form of the Trinity. It must be kept open. It must serve as a means of expressing the divine Life to humanity.

Commentary

The purpose of this commentary is not to add to an already over-heated argument concerning the nature of the three facets of the Trinity. It is, instead, meant to provide a bit of history to the

Trinitarianism concept so that the reader may better understand the nature of the controversy and alternative views of the relationship between God, Jesus and the divine Spirit.

The word Trinity is not a part of the Bible. It was first used by one of the great Apostolic Fathers, Tertullean (2nd Century), whose motive was to speak of a living God, God the Creator, Jesus the Word, and the divine Spirit, the power of God in the world. Tertullian and others perceived God as best known and understood through the nature of his great love. Within this theology all of creation, including humans, are viewed as being created good, and the Creator God is the same as the Savior God.

This contrasted dramatically with another great Apostolic Father, Origen, who conceived of a holy revolt against God in the heavens. According to Origen, the spirits in heaven:

> ...were originally equal and free, but they fell away from their unity with God in different degrees of distance. As a result of their revolt in heaven against God, they may have fallen into material bodies. This is their punishment and at the same time the way of their purification....The fall...is a transcendent fall. It precedes our existence in time and space....[21]

Origen, along with the Eastern Church in Constantinople, perceived Jesus as a demi-God, with a kind of lesser validity and power of being than the Father, they also thought this to be true of the Spirit. According to Origen, the fall, having occurred before the creation, produced a universal fallenness. Human existence and the existence of reality as a whole, therefore, are considered as a part of guilt and judgment.

[21.] Paul Tillich, *A History of Christian Thought*, (New York: Simon and Schuster, 1967), p. 60.

Fallenness penetrates through everything humans as well as the remainder of creation.

The First Council of Nicaea in 325 attempted to reconcile these and other conflicting views. Out of this meeting came what is commonly called today, the Nicene Creed, parts of which are familiar to most of Christianity. The original version follows:

> *We believe in one God, the Father Almighty, Maker of all things visible and invisible. And in one Lord, Jesus Christ, the Son of God, begotten of the Father, the only-begotten of the essence of the Father, God of God, and Light of Light, true God of true God, begotten not made, being of one substance with the Father, by whom all things were made in heaven and on earth, who for us men and our salvation came down and was incarnate and was made man. He suffered and the third day he rose again, ascended into heaven. From thence he comes to judge the quick and the dead, and in the Holy Ghost. And those who say there was a time when he was not, or he was not before he was made, and he was made out of nothing, and out of another substance or thing, or the Son of God is created or changeable, or alterable, they are condemned by the Catholic Church.*

As Tillich tells us, this did not put the issue "to bed." Since this time the controversy has raged, with some churches within the Protestant tradition breaking entirely with the Trinitarian doctrine, creating their own particular tradition. The stakes were high, however, as the very image of God was in question, a God of love and Creation or a God of sin and judgement were being debated.

Tillich recognizes that the doctrine of the Trinity is ambiguous. He believes it important that we continue to pursue a more complete understanding. But of even more importance, is the need to more fully recognize what it says to those following the Christian tradition about the ultimate truth and love of God.

Discussion

1. Why is monotheism so important to Judaism and Christianity?

2. Why do you think that Tillich sees the need for a renewal of the doctrine of the Trinity?

   Do you accept the three roles of God? Is the third role, that of the divine Spirit, an important part of your theology?

3. Why does Tillich suggest that as a result of the controversy, Protestant Christianity has reduced the "teachings of Jesus" to a source book for moral teaching? Discuss.

CHAPTER 7

History And The Search For The Kingdom Of God

Chapter Introduction

The central point of this chapter is that history, through the power of God's love, points toward a Kingdom of God. Tillich supports his idea by showing that: (1) historical processes are progressive, i.e., they move forward, (2) historical processes, although progressive, in and of themselves, have failed to provide a clear aim or purpose to history, and (3) there is, however, an aim of history, the establishment of a loving and just society—the Kingdom of God—experienced through the realm of the spirit within humans and realizable through the power of the divine Spirit.

Life and History

Humanity and history—According to Tillich, history is most important as the deliverer of memories from one generation to the other. It is not simply an unstructured collection of occurrences. It is a deliberate selection of happenings that are considered important to those who are a part of the tradition. If a particular occurrence is considered significant it will be included in history and considered a historical event, if not, it won't be included.

History began as a combination of myths, legends, sagas, and epic poetry. The ideal of a pure, unbiased historical research appears only in recent times, and even then, existing traditions and values makes it conform with the past. It does not report "naked facts" separate from their interpretation within existing tradition. This makes history, as we know it, dependent upon the writer's personal biases and belief system.

According to Tillich, the biblical records are classic examples of this. Within history, the reason behind the writing of the history is what makes a particular historical event worth including or excluding. Without purpose, all occurrences are nothing more than unrelated events. The ability to give purpose to history, to understand one's surroundings, to see meaning, or to experience the ultimate, is unique within humans. Of particular importance in this regard, is a doctrine that Tillich calls "the infinite value of every human soul." Although this doctrine is not directly biblical, Tillich believes that this was the purpose of the biblical writers.

Regarding the entire span of history, Tillich points out that it is impossible to identify the moment in time when humans gained their first spark of historical consciousness. In the same sense, we do not know at what moment in time humankind as we understand it today will cease to exist.

Tillich suggests some possibilities concerning this latter point. One possibility is that humankind will self-destruct through some form of catastrophic occurrence. This is very possible with the discovery of atomic energy and the development of a biological means of conducting war. Another possibility is that humankind will be destroyed gradually (or suddenly) by natural causes. These causes may be from either biological or physical changes taking place in the world. Another possibility, according to Tillich, is that humankind will lose its drive for discovering new things, and become essentially satisfied or at least tolerant of the human condition as it exists. Given this scenario, humans may stop "growing," becoming non-thinking clones. Tillich refers to this as a negative utopia such as that described in Alduos Huxley's classic book the *Brave New World*. These are but a few of the possibilities of how humanity may cease to exist. They must not be mixed up with the end of history, however, as envisioned in apocalyptic literature, i.e., the Bible's Book of Revelation. This is a separate matter and will be discussed later.

The rise of "communities and states" plays a special role in history, according to Tillich. Communities are characterized by their ability to act in common. In order to do this, they must have some form of centralized power that keeps individual members of the community united. This is necessary, if for no other reason, than to protect itself from confrontations with other communities. Communities must have central, law-giving, law-enforcing authority and the means necessary to repel outside attack. When these conditions are fully met, the community is commonly called a "state," and, in a very real sense, history is predominately a history of states. Although it is true that economic, cultural, and religious movements influence history; history is concerned primarily with individual states.

A state characteristically has a means of making and administering laws, although this is not the source of its political power. Its "real" political power comes from what Tillich calls "eros" (love) that produces an experience of belonging, a sense of community, and a sense of purpose within the nation. Examples of that which makes such power possible include blood (family) relations, language, tradition, common culture, and religion.

Through the use of force, power is frequently preserved and attempts are made to increase it; force, however, is not the basis for a true and lasting power. Although force is essential to the maintenance of the state, it is also the cause of the state's destruction which occurs when force is overused or when it replaces the true source of political power—eros relations.

According to Tillich, it is the eros relationship that points humanity toward a "Kingdom of God," the culmination of history.

Categories of life and history—Tillich introduces the concept of categories as another means of looking at history. There are four of particular significance: time, space, causality, and substance.

Time and space relationships vary a bit depending on the specific dimension being considered. As an example, in the organic dimension, time is time to a human as well as to an amoeba, however, a day in the life of a human may be the entire life span of an amoeba. The same relationship is true in space as well. Space is space to the human as well as to the amoeba, but a human's need for space is much greater than that of an amoeba.

In the *inorganic realm* space is the dominant category. Time is a factor but one's daily life continuously encounters the spatial solidity of physical objects. Existing in the inorganic realm means, above all, to have a place solely one's own. This is, in a sense, a form of being exclusive. Nothing else occupies the space. Exclusiveness is also found in time, as every discernable moment of time, excludes the preceding moment. As time passes, a drop of water running down a river bed is here in this moment and there the next.

In the *organic realm* a new quality of time and space appears: exclusiveness is replaced by participativeness with neither time or space predominant. The space of a tree, as an example, is not the same kind of space an inorganic rock occupies, an exclusive space, independent of all others. A tree, as an organic entity, occupies a space filled with interdependent parts such as roots, limbs, and leaves. They participate together in occupying the space. Regarding time, it is also participative. As time passes, the tree envelops its old self into its new.

Within the *realm of self-awareness*, found only in animal life, one aspect of time follows another but the element of exclusiveness of the inorganic is broken as memory (which is basic to self-awareness) overlaps memory. Regarding time and space, space is what the animal moves through as time passes. This may be very small or very large.

Within the *dimension of the spirit*, time and space relationships are characterized by Tillich as "essentially unlimited." The mind is able to overcome the limits existing in all other dimensions by rising above and beyond them. This is uniquely possible within humans and is critical to one's relationship with God. Regarding time, Tillich uses the example of a painting to illustrate his point. A painting, in an inorganic sense, has concrete limits that are expressed as the period when the painting is being created and the precise time when it is finished. This kind of time, however, cannot measure the real value of the painting. Only the spirit can do this. The spirit perceives the creativity within the painting and the context within which the painting exists, past, present, and future, particularly within such genres as Expressionistic Art. The experience of time within the spirit sees the impact that the painting may have on society within and after the period within which the painting took place.

A parallel situation occurs regarding space and the spirit. As in time, there is an element of "essentially unlimited." The spirit runs ahead, beyond a specific issue, without any limitations placed on it by the issue; in other words a sort of fantasy takes place. Limitation is involved, however, as the spirit must return to the specific issue, resolving it in concrete terms. The conquering of space by NASA is a good example of this relationship. The creative spirit runs well ahead of the practical, on to what is considered a dream of future possibilities. It must, however, return to the concrete, the production of rocket ships, which takes space.

Tillich now returns to the *dimension of history*, the subject of this chapter, suggesting that time never goes backward, it only runs ahead toward the new, the unique, and the novel, never repeating itself. Although similarities in historical events occur with frequency, every event has an element of uniqueness. Time pushing forward into the new suggests that it is running toward some form of space fulfillment. It is within this realm that one begins to see the possibility of a "Kingdom of God."

Causality (cause and effect) and substance (categories) must be discussed together as were time and space. Within *the dimension of the inorganic*, causality (which presumes a cause and effect relationship) is apparent, as an example, when a hammer (the cause) pounds a nail into a board (the effect). Substance, the other category under discussion, names (or categorizes) the cause—a hammer—and the effect—a nail in a board. They are two different things or substances.

In the *dimension of the organic*, causality and substance change both in their character and relationship to each other. Within an organism, the cause (chemical-physical processes) and effect takes place in the same organism. As an example, a plant produces food through a process called photosynthesis (the cause) and it grows in diameter and height, producing flowers (the effect). It is true that external impacts influence the cause-effect relationship but only as a trigger device. They are not the cause of the consequent effect.

In the *dimension of self-awareness* the same situation occurs; that which is within the person (the cause) produces continuous growth and development (the effects). The substance or classification of the cause and effect is the same—the person. Here again there may be a triggering device (i.e., a stimulating speech or a major experience in one's life), but the change is limited to within the self-awareness of the person.

In *the dimension of the spirit*, causality's effects are no longer imprisoned within the person. The cause (the person) results in new and creative acts (effects) outside the person. There is a new creation that is not controlled by past events in the life of the individual. The creation of great art, music, and poetry are but a few of the effects of the causal agent, the spirit of the person.

According to Tillich, the varying characteristics of causality and substance have a direct bearing on "literal" understandings of the Bible. Literalist views examine the relationship between causality and substance only in the inorganic sense. God (the cause) created the world (the effect). He considers this to be a very limiting viewpoint as it overlooks or ignores other dimensions. Within the dimension of the spirit, there is great potential for growth and creativity, particularly through the presence of the divine Spirit within the spirit of the individual.

Regarding *history*, causality and substance are both dependent on all dimensions for their interpretation. As previously discussed, communities and nations are the causal agents within much of history. They do this in two related ways. The specific nation or community (the cause) changes the culture within itself (the effect). The second way is the exact opposite of the first. The culture (cause) produces a change in the nation or community (the effect).

One major exception to this is that within the dimension of the spirit the creativity that emanates from the spirit may affect the culture in almost a revolutionary way, negating possible changes initiated by the community or nation. Historical examples, such as Hellenism, the Renaissance, the formation of Western and Eastern cultures, are good illustrations. These movements or trends are what provide much of the understanding of history.

Obviously, causality and substance have played a major role in deciding the direction that the world is taking: causality, in providing constant change, and substance, in helping us to understand the nature of the change. Humans can hope to affect this direction through a better understanding of the processes involved. According to Tillich, cause and effect relationships within the spirit point toward a new future. Within them there is a quest for a universal historical substance, a new substance, which transcends every situation. This he calls the Kingdom of God, a community in which all tensions are balanced and in complete unity with God.

The dynamics of history—Tillich discusses three issues regarding historical dynamism: (1) the effect of trends and chance, (2) the effect of structures, and (3) the effect of rhythm.

Trends and chance have a very important effect upon the direction taken by history, according to Tillich. Trends are quite obvious throughout history as we see the past projected into the future. Chance, however, never quite lets any given trend settle down.

The relationship between trends and chance is quite important. If there were no chance, trends would, in essence, become universal laws or direction, unchanging, inviolate. This never happens, according to Tillich, no matter how strong the trend. They are always changed.

Because of the relationship between trends and chance, every moment in history is new in relation to all preceding moments, while if trends were universal laws, they would demand consistent, repeatable occurrences or behaviors. Trends are quite important, however, as they do provide a degree of predictability to history.

"Chances" are defined by Tillich as constantly occurring situations that, if acted upon, may significantly change the direction trends are taking. They are unforeseeable. Once they occur, however, there must be something that happens for it to become a real "chance," otherwise, it is only a chance-giving situation. Tillich points out that the very existence of chances, precludes the possibility of any form of historical determinism such as doctrines of predestination (God foreordains everything that happens before it happens) and dialectics (all history results from the process of logical argumentation). In these movements the world is visualized as having no chance happenings.

Structural processes are defined as those processes in a society that decide the outcome of a historical event. Structural processes at work in the world result in progress, as well as regression, action as well as reaction, and growth as well as decay. Many structural processes have had an important effect upon history and the resulting trends. Unfortunately, however, they are too often, and incorrectly so, described as universal laws. According to Tillich, they are not universal laws as there simply are too many exceptions to the "rule" in each of them.

The most important structural process of all, according to Tillich, is that of dialectics (logical argumentation) as dialectics produces a stress from which much of society's creativity appears. Dialectics, or the dialectical structure of historical events, is given special consideration by Tillich. It has influenced world history more profoundly than any of the other structures, particularly through Marxist doctrine and philosophy. No matter how much one may hold Marxist doctrine and philosophy in disdain, dialectics is an important scientific tool for the analysis and description of the dynamics of life. Wherever life conflicts with itself, and through the resulting struggle a new and better way results, real dialectics takes place. However, he reminds us, that dialectics is only a process and is not a universal law as believed in Marxist philosophy. It cannot be empirically proven to be a law.

Periodic rhythms can be observed through all of history, according to Tillich. They are periods, however, only if they can be identified and defined, as there are continuous transitions, overlappings, advances and delays within history with no sign post marking one period from another. Although sometimes hard to see, they are an important way to describe or better understand the dynamics of history.

As far as Tillich is concerned, history is progressive as every creative act that may occur historically moves history toward the new. This applies to all aspects of human culture. In every group, even the most conservative, there are creative acts that produce progress. Observation of these facts has led many within society to believe that history approaches some ultimate aim or that, at a minimum, progress itself is the aim.

Tillich believes that there are realms of life that are subject to an ultimate aim. He conditions his view somewhat, however, by suggesting that in areas of activity where freedom predominates, there can be no aim. The possibility of no aim or progress may sound strange to many people, as freedom is so cherished. What Tillich is saying, however, is that it is impossible to sustain any direction or aim when individual freedom results in a society moving in all directions at the same time.

If freedom limits the possibility of progress toward an aim, the area of morality can not progress or have an aim, as freedom is fundamental to morality. This may be so, according to Tillich, he suggests, however, that we must take a closer look at morality before drawing this conclusion.

There are two forces at play in morality, moral education and moral conduct. Education provides moral progress through repetitious learning resulting in the gaining of certain desirable moral habits. Repetition involved in education conditions one to act in a prescribed manner, reducing one's freedom. This is progress. In this way, education creates mature, moral personalities and the level of moral conduct in a group increases. Where this goes awry, however, is when an individual confronts an actual moral situation that needs a specific action or conduct. The resulting conduct will occur freely even though conditioned a bit by a moral habit learned through education. Education does not dictate the response, it only conditions it.

Tillich believes that moral progress within humanity is not possible qualitatively but is possible quantitatively. Qualitatively, throughout history, there have been instances of highly moral individuals and highly just societies. These may never be exceeded except in quantitative terms. One can quantify the numbers of people developing their humanity, or the number of communities exercising higher levels of justice, which are signs of progress. Education has a major influence on this. The real issue, then, is that of quantity.

A very important question concerning historical progress, according to Tillich, is whether progress is possible in religion, not simply within that of morality. He addresses this from two perspectives: internally, through the culture that exists within religion, and externally, through the means of continuous revelatory experience.

There is progress, obsolescence, and regression within all religious culture no matter the particular faith or denomination. The degree of progress possible depends on the extent to which these cultures are open to progress. Progress is often difficult, however, as there is a great deal of inflexibility in much of the church's dogma and doctrine.

Another means of progress is through revelation. According to Tillich, the divine Spirit is and has been the same throughout history, and in this respect there is no progress in revelation. In another respect, progress is possible, and is dependent on the increased receptivity of individual humans to the power and continuous revelation of the divine Spirit. Receptivity is dependent on the totality of external and internal factors that make up one's life, such as maturity, language, study and experience. As one progresses from immaturity to maturity, revelatory experience becomes clearer and the powers of the divine Spirit more manifest.

Tillich rejects the idea that Christianity, as a religion, is absolute and that other religions are a progressive approximation to it. It is only the central event of the Christ that is absolute, not Christianity. The unique event of the Christ, and the power that this event has through the cross, serve as the criteria for judging all religions including Christianity.

Problems within the Historical Dimension of Life

The problem of empire and centralization within self-integration— History, as it moves toward its ultimate aim, continuously realizes certain intermediate aims through the process of self-integration. Intermediate aims may result in movement either toward the ultimate aim or away from it. This can readily be seen by looking at problems of empire and centralization and the changes that occur within them. Empires are the result of individuals aiming for some form of universal meaning or direction. Aiming for universal meaning has played an important role in the political history of many nations, including the church. All efforts, however, have failed as total universality has never been reached.

According to Tillich, empires are known for the disintegrative, destructive, and profanization of much that they have touched. It is impossible to imagine the amount of suffering and destruction that is inevitably connected with it, though, at times, empire has shown an integrating and creative side.

In respect to the recent past, there has been a drive toward supremacy on the part of both the United States and the Soviet Union during the cold war that is now defunct. This led to the deepest and most universal split in history, according to Tillich. To a certain extent, this has been the result of a struggle for power and dominance, though this is only a part of the reason. To a much greater extent, each nation strove to make their own particular aim or purpose universal. In the United States the driving aim was to strengthen the principle of liberty. In Russian Communism, the driving aim was a proletarian oriented, dialectic materialism.[22] The tragic consequence of this conflict was evident and it could have become the source of humanity's total destruction.

Besides the problems associated with empire, there is also the internal power struggle which takes place within groups. This needs to be looked at in respect to how a group uses its power in relation to those who belong to the group. According to Tillich, there are two distinct directions that internal power structures take: (1) toward a totalitarian control of the life of every member of the group (this is particularly evident in imperial groups), and (2) toward the encouragement of the personal freedom of every member of the group, including the encouragement of creativity.

[22.] Dialectic materialism is a system of logic used by Karl Marx to exam problems in social and economic processess. It is based on the philosopher Hegel's principle that an idea or event (thesis) generates its opposite (antithesis) leading to a reconciliation of opposites (synthesis).

Often times there is a strengthening of totalitarian control when a nation is attack from without or when those in power react to a threat from within. In both instances, a strengthened power center reduces and sometimes destroys the elements of freedom operational within the group or nation. Although the totalitarian control remains very powerful, it becomes less creative in its exercise of power. Ultimately, the dictator, or dictatorial elite, becomes so powerful, and creativity so diminished, that all meaning or purpose is lost. Without meaning or purpose, the group self- destructs as a result of revolution.

Promoting personal freedom also has its set of problems. Personal freedom is most often promoted best through the presence of multi-power centers, no one center dominating the others for any length of time. The "checks and balance" system within the United States illustrates this type of structure as it shares power between the presidency, the legislative, and the judicial arms of the government. In groups such as these, according to Tillich, the drive for personal freedom may become so strong that the multiple power centers are unable to provide essential direction to the group. As a result, the positive affects of personal freedom and creativity within the group may be seriously diminished due to a lack of a positive, meaningful direction.

Problems of revolution and reaction within self-creativity—Within the process of self-creativity, that which is new includes within it elements of the old (out of which the new grew). According to Tillich, this is important, though sometimes serious destructive forces emerge. One may see destructive forces operating in relationships between generations, in the struggles between artistic and philosophical styles, in ideologies found within political parties, in the oscillation between revolution and reaction, and in the tragic situations to which these conflicts lead. The greatness of history as it moves toward the new has within it the "seeds" of great tragedy.

As a concrete example, Tillich discusses the problem of relationships between generations. This is not a matter of authority, as far as Tillich is concerned, but a matter of the interface between the old and new. In order to make a place for themselves in the existing structures of society, the younger generation attacks the older generation. The attack by the younger generation often overlooks the fact that, at one time, the existing structures came about as a result of an attack from a younger generation. The older generation often overlooks this as well, and considers the attack unfair, uninformed, and unappreciative of the creative struggles of the past. They, in turn, fail to see that the results of their past creativity have now become stumbling blocks to new creativity. In this conflict, the older generation sometimes becomes hardened and bitter and the younger generation frustrated and combative.

Within the political realm there are many problems regarding change. Of particular importance, is whether the change generated in a political party actually results from a creative process. Possibly it is simply the result of a desire to be new and different. In this latter case, there are many instances in which one party or the other, consciously or unconsciously, distorts facts and promises future action not really intended, in order to destroy the creativity and credibility of the opposing party. This is particularly evident in clashes between so-called conservative and liberal ideologies. In the extreme, revolution—not necessarily bloody—may occur as an attempt is made to overthrow the power structure and reassert freedom and creativity. When the violence and destruction is too radical, freedom and creativity may become impossible to achieve. When the new replaces the old and comes to power, it often contradicts its original reasons for revolution—the providing of freedom.

The problems of the "third stage" as given and as expected within self-transcendence—The conflicts between the old and the new reach their most destructive stage when either side claims the ultimate word for itself. A claim of ultimacy has happened in both the political (e.g., Nazi Germany) and in the religious sphere. The struggle between the sacred old and the prophetic new has been a central theme in religious history and has led to religious wars and persecution.

Many different groups have claimed to represent the aim of history either in terms of its actual or anticipated fulfillment. The "third stage"—restoration—is the traditional symbol used for the aim of history. Paradise is the first stage, the fall is the second stage, and the third stage restoration follows.

According to one early church father, Augustine, the third stage began with the foundation of the Christian church. Others disagree with this, claiming that the third stage has yet to come. Secular society sees the rise of the bourgeoisie, the middle class, and the rise of the proletariat, the working industrial class, as symbols of the third stage. Whether in religious or secular terms, according to Tillich, the general conviction is that the third stage has started. History has reached a point that cannot be reversed. The "beginning of the end" is at hand. With many, the ultimate fulfillment of history can be seen, the Kingdom of God.

The problems of the individual—According to Tillich, the political process, not the individual, directs the path of history. The political process forms the power centers of a society and controls the direction that society takes. This is why much of recorded history is the history of political personalities and their actions, rather than artists, scientists, and theologians.

Within the democratic institutions of the political realm, according to Tillich, one can best see the predominance of the political function and its relationship to the individual. Democracy makes possible the fight for freedom. This fight, however, has many problems. The techniques for representation are imperfect, "power brokers" wield influence far beyond their constituencies. The average person perceives party politics as mysterious and uninfluenceable by other than the wealthy and powerful. Channels of public communications, and sophisticated techniques of forming "desirable" public opinion, become instruments of a conformity that suppresses creativity as successfully as dictators. Democracy has the potential of becoming unworkable because of the rise of too many parties, or because disruptive splits within parties, so that a majority capable of action becomes impossible. This may occur to such a degree that essential or advisable political action is impossible.

Unfortunately, the individual observing these occurrences does not see a process leading toward a greater society, or a transcendent aim, but rather a society full of broken political promises, a history of political "tugs of war" over issues they are unable to affect themselves or issues not important to the life they would hope to live. Within individuals there is a widespread indifference and feelings of cynicism and power-lessness. The symbols of hope, in both the secular and religious realms, have lost their power to move one beyond the existing into a new and exciting future, according to Tillich. The world has become "old."

Although Tillich acknowledges that democracy is far superior to any other system of governing known, it does not resolve the problem of whether there is or is not an ultimate meaning or direction in history.

Interpretations of History:
The Search for the Kingdom of God

The meaning of history: problems—According to Tillich, a person may look at history in one of two ways, either non-historically or historically. The non-historical way presumes that history has no ultimate purpose or direction. This is the belief of the largest number of human beings. Those who hold this view, according to Tillich, look at the non-historical meaning through what he calls the tragic, the mystical, and the mechanistic interpretations.

The *tragic* interpretation, strong in classical Greek thought, sees history running in circles, always coming back to its beginning. Each circle had as its beginning a time of greatness followed by decay and destruction and then another beginning. One saw and appreciated the glories of life in nature, nations and people, and deplored the misery and tragic quality of life. However, within the tragic conception there is no hope or expectation of a transcendent historical fulfillment.

The *mystical* interpretation of history is strongest in Vedanta Hinduism, Taoism and in Buddhism, according to Tillich, although it is also found in western culture in the philosophical schools of Neoplatoism and Spinozism. In this interpretation, historical existence has no meaning. One must live in it and act reasonably, but history itself can neither create anything new nor can there be anything truly and permanently real. There is no awareness of historical time and an end toward which it is running. There is no drive to transform history into the direction of universal humanity and justice. The problems of life are seen as unconquerable. The only existence possible is to transcend life's problems and living as though one has already returned to the Ultimate One. Although there is no symbol analogous to the Kingdom of God, there is often great compassion for those who are suffering in the world.

Finally, the *mechanistic* interpretation of history is found within modern science. History is nothing more than a series of happenings in the physical universe, interesting to investigate and record, but without any special contribution to the meaning of existence. It is closely related to the technical control of nature by science and technology. This gives it a progressive character only if one believes humans can improve on nature more than they produce destructive consequences.

We have been discussing the non-historical interpretation of history. Tillich now turns to a historical interpretation, dividing his discussion between progressivism and transcendence. The significant thrust of *progressivism* is the view that there is a progressive intention behind every creative act. If this be so, there are two distinct directions toward which this belief may take one, belief in an infinite progress without an ultimate fulfillment, and a belief in a progress leading to ultimate fulfillment. This latter form is called utopianism.

Progressivism, as infinite progress without ultimate fulfillment, has its roots in the philosophical school of Neo-Kantianism and permeates the ideal of modern industrial society. According to Tillich, infinite progress is possible, particularly in the field of technological creativity. Scientifically speaking there is much evidence providing a scientific justification of progress as a universal law of history. In the twentieth century, however, the world has had relapses into stages of inhumanity supposedly overcome long ago. There have also been increased feelings of meaninglessness that have surfaced because of progress without end, along with an increase in frustration concerning how each newborn human seems to start over in its freedom to pursue either good or evil. The lessons of history need constant re-enforcement. This has resulted in a radical breakdown in progressivism as people begin to believe that the world is on a "down-hill" path.

Progressivism, as infinite progress with ultimate fulfillment, or what is often called the utopian ideal, has provided the sharpest attack on progressivism as-infinite-progress without ultimate fulfillment, according to Tillich. Utopianism is progressivism with a definite aim: an aim culminating in a stage of history within which all problems of life are over. In utopianism, humanity will create an actual paradise on earth. Much of the utopian impetus came from that period of history called the Renaissance (14th through the 16th century) and was then carried forward into this century. According to Tillich, many elements of the utopian ideal have appeared, only to regress in those areas dependent upon humanity's freedom of choice, as choices are made not consistent to the ideals of utopianism. There has been a profound disappointment accompanying this regression, and a history of cynicism, mass indifference, fanaticism, and tyranny has resulted. According to Tillich, this is to be expected, as utopianism, taken literally, is idolatrous—it has been made a god. It ignores the fact of human estrangement and the problems of life and history. This makes the utopian interpretation of history inadequate and dangerous.

Transcendence, or an existence focusing on a heavenly world, is another form of inadequate historical interpretation of history that involves an ultimate aim. Very little historical action is possible. According to Tillich, this interpretation is based on two distinct worlds, the heavenly world and the earthly world. No relationship exists in transcendence between the justice of the Kingdom of God in heaven and the justice of human beings and their respective power structures in the world. There is no place for revolutionary attempts to change a corrupt political system. According to Tillich, the attitude expressed in these ideas fits the demands of essentially powerless people who have given up the possibility of improving their situation on earth. Their trust is placed in a future heaven.

This idea has had some relevancy in all periods of history, including today. Theologically, it serves to counterbalance utopianism, but, as in utopianism, it too is inadequate. Its most obvious shortcoming is that it concentrates exclusively on the salvation of the individual and ignores the possibility of transforming the historical group and the universe into a Kingdom of God. The Kingdom of God is understood as a static, supernatural order, into which individuals enter after their death, and it ignores the dynamic power of the Lord's Prayer regarding a Kingdom of God in the world:

> *Our Father who art in heaven, hallowed be thy name, thy kingdom come thy will be done on earth as it is in heaven. Matthew 6:9-10.*

The meaning of history is the Kingdom of God—Closely related to each other, and in certain respects identical, are the symbols: divine Spirit, Kingdom of God, and Eternal Life. Although parallel symbols,

Tillich, differentiates between them. The symbol divine Spirit is that which addresses the problems of the human spirit, the Kingdom of God is that which addresses the problems of history, and Eternal Life is that symbol which addresses the ambiguities of life itself.

According to Tillich, the Kingdom of God is more encompassing than the other two. It has two aspects to its meaning, one of which is inner-historical (within history) and the other trans-historical (beyond history). Inner-historically, the Kingdom of God is the ultimate aim of history, and is realized through the activity of the divine Spirit. Trans-historically, the Kingdom of God has arrived, and is identical with Eternal Life. These two aspects of the Kingdom of God make it most important to Christian thought, particularly when one considers that the preaching of Jesus started with "...for the Kingdom of Heaven is at hand." (Matthew 4:17) and the Lord's Prayer includes the petition "...thy kingdom come..." (Matthew 6:10). Unfortunately, according to Tillich, the symbol Kingdom of God has largely been pushed aside by Christianity. It has lost its power as a result of a partially secularized social gospel movement and through some forms of religious socialism.

The Kingdom of God's reinstatement as a living symbol may come about from an encounter between some of the Eastern religions (in particular Buddhism) with Christianity, although Tillich sees some problems with this. Buddhism claims to accept every religion as partial truth through Buddhism's self-transcendent universality. It seems impossible to Tillich, however, that it can accept the symbol Kingdom of God with its personal, social, and political spheres. These are fundamental to the understanding of the symbol Kingdom of God and the Christian experience and they are transcended and never dealt with in Buddhism. The consequences of these differences, according to Tillich, can have worldwide importance as both religions interchange the basis of their respective faiths.

Tillich addresses additional problems through a discussion of what he considers to be four distinct characteristics of the Kingdom of God:

the political, social, personal and universal. The *political* characteristic he has already discussed. The *social* characteristic includes the ideas of peace and justice. The inclusion of God in this characteristic excludes the possibility of a world totally fulfilled as a result of humankind alone. It adds the dimension of holiness, and the moral imperative of love, which serve as the foundations to peace and justice. The *personal* characteristic gives eternal meaning to the individual in contrast to the Buddhist Nirvana, which symbolizes the absorption of the individual soul into the supreme spirit. And finally, the characteristic of *universality* involves the fulfillment of all life, including all of nature.

The symbol, Kingdom of God, is both operational within history and, at the same time, transcends history. Emphasized in the Bible's messages is the involvement of the Kingdom of God within the world's history. Judaism is the medium through which one is to gain an understanding of God's character and action. The true God, the God of justice, conquers the demonic forces in the world. History, however, has shown that the Kingdom of God has not arrived as a result of God's involvement. The Romans destroyed Israel, dispersed the Jews, the Jews coming together again only quite recently. Political upheavals continue throughout the world. The threat of total world annihilation continues.

Experiences such as these, according to Tillich, have changed the emphasis from God active in the world to a transcendent Kingdom of God. This began in the so-called apocalyptic literature of the period between the Old and New Testaments, with some predecessors in the latest parts of the Old Testament. According to this literature, the earth has become old, and demonic powers are in control. According to the New Testament, wars, disease, and natural catastrophes will precede the rebirth of all things and the second coming of Christ will usher in a new eon. Through a new eon, there will be peace between nations, including nature, so that most hostile species of animals, as the Old Testament tells us, will live peacefully beside each other:

...The wolf also shall dwell with the lamb, and the leopard shall lie down with the kid..." Isaiah 11:6

The Messiah, the Christ, will usher in the new eon. This vision of a new eon is obviously far removed from a Kingdom of God as we know it within history. The New Testament adds this dimension with the appearance of Jesus the Christ in the world, and the beginning of the church's involvement within history. These developments show that the symbol Kingdom of God has the power to express both the inner and the transcendent activity of God. With this in mind, Tillich discusses the reality of the Kingdom of God in and above history in the remaining sections of his systematic theology.

Commentary

Is history truly progressive? Does history have an aim? Answers to these two questions vary considerably within the Christian church. There are those churches who concentrate on the second coming of Christ in anticipation of a glorious heaven, meanwhile, tolerating the current conditions of the world. Others perceive a war taking place between the forces of good (Christians) and those of evil (Satan) with the winner "take all," though faith has only one victor, the Christian. And others, as does Tillich, perceive a loving God, one who bestows freedom of thought and action on all of humanity, expecting and assisting individuals in the development of their human potential within God's love on earth as well as through all of eternity. Within this latter view, the Kingdom of God resides in the spirit of humans who are committed to the full realization of a historical aim, the Kingdom of God on earth.

Many theologians and much of the Protestant church, share Tillich's vision of the present and the future Kingdom of God. In its own way, business and government in this country, as well as most other industrial societies, are applying management principles consistent with God's bestowal of freedom on all humanity. Frederick Herzberg, an industrial psychologist, describes the situation faced in much of society today:

> *One's ability to compare one's situation with that of another, and to score one's situation with that of another, and to score one's self as less than one's fellow worker because one makes less money, has a smaller car and has less status, causes one to suffer greatly. Thus it is apparent that the human capacity to be unhappy is inexhaustible, because the range of stimuli that can cause pain to humankind is so vast and the number of situations in which a person can make comparisons is equally inexhaustible.[23]*

Within the framework of this reality, Herzberg suggests a motivation-hygiene concept achievable within the framework of businesses and governmental institutions.[24] This concept identifies two sets of needs within people: the animal need to avoid pain and the human need to grow psychologically. Herzberg hypothesizes that if management's energies go exclusively toward avoiding pain (e.g., providing employees health benefits or higher wages), the net result is to keep people from hurting, or to keep them from being dissatisfied. Efforts such as these are what he calls hygienic. They do not produce wholeness. Herzberg does not discount the need for hygienic approaches by management which keep people from getting sick; he suggests, however, that hygiene alone does not produce health. Health occurs only when humans are also provided the opportunity (freedom) to grow psychologically by exercising freedom and initiative in their job. Within

---

23. Frederick Herzberg, *Work and the Nature of Man* (Cleveland: The World Publishing Company, 1966), p.49.

24. Herzberg, pp. 49-54, 71-79.

Tillich's theology, Herzberg introduces a process that leads toward those values encompassed in a Kingdom of God.

Pomeroy, in his book applying Tillich's theology to the world of work and family suggests that:

> *there is an emerging consciousness in the United States that management, through collaborativeness and participation of employees, is capable of providing a quality of results significantly higher than the more familiar autocratic, power oriented leadership.*[25]

Douglas McGregor, psychologist, has meaningfully helped raise the consciousness level of this style of management with a Theory Y management concept, based upon the integration of an individual employee's goals and the goals of the employer. Integration is accomplished, simply stated, through involving an employee in the decisions that affect what he or she is doing. McGregor suggests that:

> *Above all, the assumptions of Theory Y point up the fact that the limits on human collaboration in the organizational setting are not limits of human nature, but of management's ingenuity in discovering how to realize the potential represented by its human resources.*[26]

This indeed is a precursor of the Kingdom of God.

[25.] Richard Pomeroy, In Search of Meaning (Berkeley: The Glen Berkeley Press, 1991). p.62.

[26.] Douglas McGregor, The Human Side of Enterprise (New York: McGraw Hill, 1960) p.45.

Discussion

1. What are the implications of what Tillich calls "the infinite value of every soul?" as it relates to "heaven" and "hell?"

2. Tillich tells us that it is "eros" relationships that point toward a Kingdom of God. Why do you think he believes this? Do you agree?

3. How does one's view of God and the Kingdom vary as viewed from different dimensions of life? What are the implications for the church?

4. Do you agree that progress in morality is possible only quantitatively?

5. Are we in the "third stage" of world history? What does this mean to you? Be as specific as possible.

6. Is there an observable progress in history?

7. Is there an aim to history? If so, what is it? If not, why?

CHAPTER 8

The Kingdom Of God Within History

Chapter Introduction

The major thrust of this chapter is that Jesus (not the Christian religion) is the "center of history" and, as such, serves as the criterion for identifying all that is truly holy and righteous. All that happened before the advent of Jesus was in preparation for his arrival (the Old Testament), all that has occurred since his arrival is meant to better understand his meaning (the New Testament). Tillich tells us that it is only the Christian church that contains within itself the essence of life, Jesus the Christ, and, as such, is elevated above all other religions. The church represents, although imperfectly, the ultimate truth and value revealed through Jesus. In suggesting this, Tillich recognizes that all religions, including Christianity, are subject to greatness as well as demonization. They are all exalted and profane, divine and demonic.

Tillich separates the functions of the church into two general areas: (1) transcendentally, in lifting the world beyond itself toward God, and (2) working within the world in the struggle of the Kingdom of God against the forces of demonization and a secular society. Tillich calls this latter category the "fighting church," which uses the power of the divine Spirit as its means to affect social justice in the world and the Kingdom of God in one's heart.

History and Jesus the Christ

Jesus the Christ as the center of history—According to Tillich, the appearance of Jesus the Christ as the "center of history" is crucial to Christianity. The word "center" as used here, refers to that moment in history in which everything before the arrival of Jesus is in preparation for his arrival (i.e., the Old Testament), and everything after his arrival is devoted to understanding its meaning (i.e., the New Testament). The expression "center of history" has nothing to do with the number of years that went by before or after his arrival.

Tillich tells us that theologically speaking, no progress within an individual is possible beyond that already revealed in Jesus as the Christ. The only progressivism possible is humankind's progress from immaturity to maturity, and the increased understanding of Jesus as history's central event. Humankind had to mature to a point that Jesus as the Christ could be understood upon his arrival. This has been a function of the Old Testament. Without the Old Testament, Christianity would retreat into the immaturities of other religions, including Judaism, whose history the Old Testament prophets highly criticized. An important point here, is that this maturing process goes on today as it did in the pre-Christian epoch.

The history of the Christian church begins with the arrival of Christ. The church not only acquires the truths of the past through the Christ but also, through Christ, foresees what will happen in the future if individuals and their institutions follow or do not follow the way of life that Christ has revealed. This has no relationship to predicting specific future events, it simply describes what the consequences would be if one does not follow the way of Jesus the Christ. If this is ignored, one's development is limited. According to Tillich, this is the meaning of prophecy in the sense of announcing the future. It is also the meaning of those passages in the Gospel of John that points out that Jesus, as the Christ, has been present in all history:

"...in the beginning was the Word: the Word was with God and the Word was God....The Word was made flesh, he lived among us..." (John 1:1, 1:14).

Besides Christianity, there are many other religious and secular movements that claim to be the "center of history." In imperial movements, previously discussed, the motivation or desire that drives the group toward imperialism is seen as the central point of history. The flight of the Israelites from Egyptian slavery to freedom in the Promised Land, the founding of the Roman Republic, and the Revolutionary War in America are centers of their particular histories. All the world's religions lay claim to a center of history as the event that founded them. This is true of Hinduism, Islam, Buddhism, Zoroastrianism, Manichism, as well as Judaism and Christianity.

Christianity, in spite of all of this, claims to be "the universal" center of history. This is deservedly so, according to Tillich, as no other religion or movement addresses the human condition and the ambiguities of history as does Christianity. As an example, Judaism with its prophetic and apocalyptic messages, talks only to the matter of an expected "Messiah," nothing more. No new Judaic "center of history" has emerged since that of the Exodus. In Islam, the emphasis is on a law that serves as an educational vehicle but not as a "center of history." In fact, through their emphasis on the law, both Judaism and Islam serve as something of a barrier to the full understanding of Christ as the center of history. Only in Christianity is the matter of historical aim or purpose, a Kingdom of God, addressed.

Providence—One must not understand providence in a deterministic way, as though there was some divine design that controls the general course of history. A design such as this, if it is to be carried out, must include all the detail needed to assure that it is accomplished. This includes God's entering into the world when necessary, and personally orchestrating specific events. This is simply not so, according to Tillich. The immensities of moral and physical evil and the overwhelming presence of sin and its consequences, have always argued against the presence of a pre-determined providence. If there were a providence such as this, it could not ignore this situation. Even the Old Testament prophets did not provide a picture of a divinely orchestrated providence. Their prophecy concentrated on what the consequences would be if one does not follow the commandments of God.

The Kingdom of God and the Churches

The churches as the representatives of the Kingdom of God—As the representatives of the Kingdom of God, the churches represent, not only the Spiritual Community, but all of life as well though they have many problems in representing the Kingdom of God, particularly when the church often represents the demonic. This has been previously discussed. The power of the church, although it may be mis-applied, continues regardless.

Just as humans, the bearers of the spirit, cannot cease to be such, so the churches cannot cease to be representatives of the Kingdom of God, no matter how much they may fall short of the Kingdom. The churches function as representatives in two ways, according to Tillich: (1) transcendentally, in lifting the world beyond itself toward God, and (2) working within the world, in the struggle of the Kingdom of God against the forces of demonization and a secular society.

The Christian Church in its original self-interpretation was well aware of this double task, expressing it quite conspicuously in its liturgical (public worship) life. It even asked the newly baptized to separate themselves publicly from the demonic forces to which they had been subjected in their pagan past. Many contemporary churches in the act of "confirmation" take the younger generation into the ranks of the fighting church—one that works for peace and justice in the world.

At the same time, all churches have spoken of the coming of the Kingdom and the duty of everyone to be prepared for it. Unfortunately, according to Tillich, many churches have reduced this latter vision of the "coming of the Kingdom" to an individual "born again" experience. Often times there is no attention paid to the church which "fights" for a Kingdom of God on earth through the power of the divine Spirit.

In the struggle of the Kingdom of God against the forces of demonization and a secular society, the church draws power from its vision and consciousness of the "end," which is the Kingdom of God some day encompassing the entire world. Meanwhile the churches serve as a means through which the Kingdom of God becomes increasingly a part of the world, through the presence of the divine Spirit within the spirit of individual members. The New Being's power enables the church to become a fighting agent of the Kingdom of God. In addition, there is also a latent church made up of groups outside the organized churches. The latent church also includes within it the power of the New Being and has been operational in all of history, including that period before the advent of the Christ. According to Tillich:

> .... *There are youth alliances, friendship groups, educational, artistic, and political movements, and, even more obviously, individuals without any visible relation to each other in whom the Spiritual Presence's impact is felt, although they are indifferent or hostile to all overt expressions of religion. They do not belong to a church, but they are not excluded from the Spiritual Community. It is impossible to deny this if one looks at the manifold instances of profanization and demonization of the Spiritual Community in those groups—the churches—which*

claim to be the Spiritual Community. Certainly the churches are not excluded from the Spiritual Community, but neither are their secular opponents....[27]

A major role of the church is its fight against demonic and secularizing forces. This presents a problem as, at the same time, they are themselves susceptible to demonization and secularization. The paradox of the church is that they are exalted and profane, divine and demonic. The churches fight against the demonic and the profane within society as well as within themselves. Internal fights within the church lead to reform movements that are conspicuous in history. It is the fact of reformation, however, that gives churches the right to consider themselves as leaders against demonization and profanization. Few secular organizations demonstrate the ability to judge themselves as does the church.

The Kingdom of God and the history of the churches—Some claim that there was only one "true" church up to 500 A.D. or 1500 A.D., the year depending upon one's viewpoint. The Anglican church of today (i.e., the Church of England) is inclined to accept the first five hundred years (up to 500 A.D.), as superior to all other periods of church history. They then perceive themselves as closer to the "true church" then others, because of their similarity to the early church.

In contrast, the Roman Catholic church attributes to itself an absoluteness, as "the church," in every period of history up to the present time. The Greek Orthodox and the Protestant churches, generally, differ with both, as they claim their particular absoluteness through

---

[27.] Tillich, III, p.153. Throughout Tillich's theology the terms divine Spirit, New Being, Spiritual Community and Spiritual Presence are used somewhat interchangeably. For reasons of clarity, this book does not use the term Spiritual Presence. For an exact definition of each term turn to the glossary at the front of this book.

various means of interpreting history. According to Tillich, each of the above interpretations is wrong. All churches are "the church" if they confess as their foundation the Christ, the central manifestation of the Kingdom of God in history. Tillich tells us that we must look at church history with the understanding that at no point is the church identical with, or totally without, elements of the Kingdom of God.

There are many unanswered riddles within the church's paradoxical nature. Chief among these are the conflicts between the church's role as the central manifestation of the Kingdom of God and the reality of church history. For example, why was the vast majority of the spread of Christianity limited to one section of the world (the Western World)? Why is it that there is seemingly such a need for so many secular movements that try to assume the traditional role of the churches? Often times, these secular institutions have turned against Christianity, as in scientific humanism and naturalistic communism. These same institutions also seem to have tremendous power in some non-Christian nations. Why?

Regarding the church's inner development and growth, there are great differences between them as various denominations grow in different directions in their approach to Christian doctrine and liturgical practice. One or the other (or all of them) claiming, in some manner, that their way is "right" and that they are "the church." Many believe that the differences are without possibility of healing. Liturgical ritualization as well as secularization plays a major role in some churches, serving as obstacles toward progress.

According to Tillich, making the divine secular is one of the great puzzles of church history. The early church absorbed the secular culture of Hellenism and Rome, using it in a manner that often enhanced the message of the Christ. In recent times, however, the secular world has not enhanced the message of Christ, a major example of this is the secularization of the birth of Jesus as shown by the intense commercialization of Christmas.

Finally, Tillich raises the question of the demonization of the church itself. The Apostle Paul in Romans, Chapter 8, proclaims the victory of Christ over the demonic powers. In spite of this, there are major demonic elements in church doctrine and dogma. Too many churches have also confused their purpose of being with the buildings they have built, which they spend so much time, money and thought maintaining.

According to Tillich, demonization within church history has been a common event. Initially there was the persecution of heretics. Then came various doctrines or formulas of condemnation in the great church councils, the inquisitions of the Middle Ages, the tyranny of Protestant orthodoxy, the fanaticism of some religious sects, the stubbornness and "tunnel vision" of fundamentalists, and the declaration of infallibility by the Pope. These are but a few examples.

In spite of all this, the church has one quality nothing else has: It contains the essence of all life, Jesus the Christ. The New Being in Jesus as the Christ elevates the Christian church above all other religions or groups in secular life. Not because they are better, but because they have a better criterion, Jesus the Christ, with which to judge and reform themselves. The struggle for the Kingdom of God is not only dramatically present in church reformation; it is also in the daily lives of individuals and communities.

The Kingdom of God and World History

The church and world history—According to Tillich, one major element divides church history from all other histories. Churches, in their judgment of the world's distorted and evil ways, include themselves within that judgement, thus providing the possibility of reformation. No other institution does this.

The churches' duality of judgment, judging the use of power in the world as well as themselves, provides them a special power. Who is better able to judge the problems of power in the world than those who recognize the misuse of power within themselves? The real test, however, is whether the churches have truly judged their own use of power, before judging others.

As an example, the Catholic judgment against communism, however justified it may be, necessarily evoked suspicion that it was based on competition between two competing powers. Protestantism is also subject to some of the same criticism. Protestant judgment is subject to the question of whether its criticisms are based on furthering humanity's ultimate aim, or as a means of furthering its own political-economic goals. This is sometimes seen in the support of a particular political movement, as in the alliance of fundamentalism and ultra-conservatism in the United States.

Tillich argues that the churches during the last 2000 years have transformed the West by changing the climate of social relationships, in particular, those between individual persons. It is true that there may be many, or even a majority, of persons that have not been directly affected by the church (the precise quality and quantity of this effect is unknown). It is also true, however, that the majority of persons have at least been exposed to affirmative ways of relating to others.

Tillich suggests that perhaps the main contribution churches have made to world history is that they produce an uneasy conscience in those who have received the New Being but still follow the old ways. Christian civilization is not the Kingdom of God; it is simply a reminder of it.

The Kingdom of God and historical self-integration: the use of power—Tillich begins his discussion of power by identifying divine power as that which is able to resist the demonic or evil.

Because democratic processes resist the misuse of power, they are seen by many as divine and, as such, a part of the Kingdom of God. This is not so, according to Tillich, they are not divine and a part of the Kingdom of God, for no matter how much democratic institutions resist the demonic, they are still fraught with misuse. Confusion on this point has led to the substitution of the idea of democracy for the symbol "Kingdom of God." This is in error.

The church's judgment against power politics, according to Tillich, should not be based on a rejection of power. It should be an affirmation of power and its proper use to correct injustice when necessary. It is carried out through prophetic witness and the judgment of institutions that are using power in a manner destructive of human potentialities. The church, in its use of power, should never attempt to control or become a part of political power. It should never force a particular political solution (e.g., communism or capitalism, for example), in the name of the Kingdom of God. One must remember that churches themselves, are not a part of the Kingdom of God.

Tillich suggests that the use of power is appropriate in disputes between individuals and groups, for example, nations. Power is inherently a part of every group as it is with every individual. The inappropriate use of power, however, is subject to question, not the power itself. According to Tillich, in a struggle between nations, the complete political defeat of one of the nations may be a significant occurrence within the Kingdom of God. This has occurred throughout Jewish history, in India's liberation from the British, and quite often in ancient Greek history. In the opposite vein, a military defeat may be the way in which the Kingdom of God deprives groups from exercising demonic claims of power—as in Hitler's Germany. Tillich suggests, that even though Hitler's defeat may be construed as a manifestation of the Kingdom of God, it does not follow that the victors, themselves, are a manifestation of God.

Tillich raises a series of questions concerning the church's attitude toward power. Must the church be pacifist, overlooking or denying the necessity of power to correct injustice? Should the church ever support a militaristic regime that believes in achieving the unity of humankind through conquest of the world? Is there some position between these two extremes for a church as representative of the Spiritual Community? Within the framework of these extremes, he believes in what is commonly called a "just" war. This is a war in which the end values (e.g., increased justice) are greater than the cost of the war with its human misery and loss of life. The American Civil and Revolutionary Wars are examples of "just" wars. Tillich recognizes, however, that it takes a daring faith to determine whether a war is just. The difficulty involved in this determination does not justify one's avoidance of the issue, however.

In spite of his belief in the concept of a "just war," Tillich believes that the church must take a pacifist viewpoint as a representative of the Spiritual Community. It is inconceivable to Tillich, that the churches could maintain themselves as representatives of the Spiritual Community and, at the same time, use military or economic weapons as tools for spreading the message of the Christ. They should, however, be political activists, supporting groups and individuals who try symbolically to represent the "Peace of the Kingdom of God" as do the Quakers and individuals such as conscientious objectors.

The Kingdom of God and historical self-creativity: social growth— Within historical self-creativity, problems of social growth rather than power are involved. Conflict arises because of the relation of the new to the old: the new involves revolution or change, and the old is based on tradition. A victory of the Kingdom of God creates unity between the new and the old. Unity is not overcome through ignoring or resisting a valuable tradition or a revolution. Tillich tells us that the status quo, or anti-revolutionary, "don't shake the boat" positions of many groups is wrong, whether the revolution (cultural or political) is unbloody or bloody. The chaos following any kind of revolution can be creative and is essential for significant progress.

Tillich does not suggest, however, that all revolutions are a part of the Kingdom of God—most certainly they are not. As an example, the fulfillment of the Kingdom of God cannot be forced on a society by destroying all cultural and political structures through a Christian revolution to end all revolutions. According to Tillich, the Apostle Paul speaks against such revolution in Chapter 13 of his letter to the Roman Church, when he tells the church to obey authority.

What is the criterion, then, to judge whether a revolution is a part of the Kingdom of God? Tillich tells us that the criterion is met when the relation between revolution and tradition mesh so that creative solutions are found. By their nature, democratic institutions try to unite conflicting sides. Democratic institutions are particularly effective when they are so structured that leaders, who do not foster unity, can be removed by legal means. Tillich cautions, however, that democratic institutions are only one way of uniting tradition and revolution. We must not forget that democratic institutions are subject to the problems inherent in the institution itself. If not properly instituted, the democratic institutions may not be able to make appropriate decisions, or, the reverse, they may become autocratic and destructive of freedom and creativity.

The Kingdom of God is just as hostile to established conformity as it is to irresponsible revolution. Conformity is a major issue with Tillich. His assessment of the history of the church is that it has stood overwhelmingly on the side of conservative-traditionalism. There are exceptions, such as the Jewish prophets, Jesus, and the Apostles, and various church reformers. Through church history one may observe that as the church becomes increasingly tradition-bound, a prophetic attack may occur from within or without. This is the power of the divine Spirit at work.

The Kingdom of God and historical self-transcendence—The Kingdom of God is victorious when there is a union between the transcendent coming of the Kingdom of God and the actual Kingdom of God as it exists imperfectly in the world today. According to Tillich, it is easy to understand the need for this union. Keeping the union dynamic, however, is difficult without letting it deteriorate into a middle way—status quo relationships of ecclesiastical or secular satisfaction. Status quoism, which avoids the issue of working toward a "Kingdom of God" on earth, results in adherents that can only "hope for the future," or "in the next life," as nothing more is possible in this life. The adherents have lost their dynamism.

Status quo relationships are not wrong in and of themselves, except that they may overlook or ignore the reality that the conditions under which they live today are not all that good. If the current reality of living is ignored, today's world may simply be tolerated, while one concentrates on individual salvation and a future life. When this happens, social action on the part of the church is often overlooked or neglected.

The implication of this for the churches is that the union between the future and the current must be kept dynamic. Without this, some churches will emphasize the present and ignore the future, while others will emphasize future expectations and salvation, ignoring the need for social transformation today.

The Kingdom of God and the individual—The Kingdom of God is victorious when individuals, as they struggle for reunion with God, do so through an active involvement in creating a Kingdom of God on earth. The more one is involved the larger the personal sacrifice. According to Tillich, the sacrifice must be one that is fulfilling to the person. To be other than fulfilling is not a sacrifice but is rather self-annihilation. The sacrifice must include a purpose that is in some manner self- fulfilling. It may be glory, as emphasized in ancient Greece; or honor, as in medieval feudal cultures. In religion, it may be to the glory of God, union with the ultimate one, or Eternal Life. Wherever sacrifice and personal fulfillment are united in this way, a victory of the Kingdom of God has taken place. The participation of the individual has received an ultimate meaning.

Commentary

Although in substantial agreement with Tillich regarding power, there is one aspect of power not addressed, the nature of the divine Spirit's power. Through my own experience I have discovered a powerful alternative to the coercive power so often relied upon today, that is the power of love as manifested in the divine Spirit. Coercive power, used in stopping Hitler is most valuable in stopping an injustice or future injustice, but it does not replace it automatically with justice.

The power of the divine Spirit, in contrast, is one of love, it is a persuasive power, one that creates justice. The following personal experience illustrates the power of persuasion versus coercion.

In 1971 I was transferred to the San Francisco Office of the Forest Service from its office in Portland, Oregon, as the director of personnel in California. Almost immediately upon arrival I found myself enmeshed in numerous controversies between my staff and field offices and between individual staff members that worked for me. The net result was poor performance and morale within the staff group of perhaps 40 people. This, of course, wasn't the most inspiring way to land in a new job, and for some long period of time I used every bit of coercive organizational power to resolve differences with little or no affect. It was obvious that I had my work cut out for me. Perhaps, as a result of the frustration within the staff, it was decided that a new strategy of change had to be created. What we had been doing simply did not work. It was at this point that we decided that "if we couldn't change the current operating climate we could at least define the type of organization we would like to be." This would at least give us a start. A few of the more than 30 characteristics we identified are as follows:

1. *All work groups will have a strong affirmative work relationship with other members of the same group, as well as with clients. Conflicts and differences are valued for their strengths.*

2. *All members of the staff are highly skilled in communication and human interaction. The staff is, collectively, valued for its advice and counsel throughout the region and at the Washington office.*

3. *The staff will help clients work out ways of solving their problems rather than telling them simply what they cannot do.*

4. *A management climate is created where people have a sense of achievement and recognition.*

5. *Create a climate where it is understood that mistakes are made, and when realized they are resolved informally and quickly and seen as a part of the development process.*

6. *Win/lose relationships or occurrences are not valued. Only win/win are valued.*[28]

What happened? We began, for the first time, to provide leadership to the region in a meaningful and productive manner. The staff, having been involved in defining the future, began to act the way that they agreed was consistent with a healthy and meaningful future. They did this of there free will, not as a result of coercive direction, but as the result of a work climate that fostered responsible freedom. Looking at it theologically, it was the power of the divine Spirit at work within our staff.

Tillich tells us that when Christians involve themselves in creating the Kingdom of God a struggle takes place in which sacrifice is involved on the part of the Christian. The more the involvement, the more the sacrifice. Though this is undoubtably true on the part of many, it certainly was not true in realizing (unknowingly) the trap-

---

[28.] Richard Pomeroy, *In Search of Meaning*, (Berkeley: Glen-Berkeley Press, 1991) p.29.

pings of the Kingdom when we defined the new organizational climate as described. It was an exciting experience.

Norman Cousins provides an added dimension to the "sacrifices" of Albert Schweitzer, one of the great personalities of this century. In his book, *Albert Schweitzer's Mission: Healing and Peace,* Cousins tells of how Schweitzer (organist, organ-builder, Bach scholar, theologian, philosopher, author, medical doctor, and Nobel Peace Prize winner) "sacrificed fortune for service when he founded his hospital in Africa. Schweitzer is described as a fascinating man, hard driving, sometimes autocratic, with an overpowering need to do good, a man who spent his Nobel Peace Prize money on a leper village.

According to Cousins, Schweitzer's "self-sacrifice" and service to others was not based on a denial (or sacrifice), but it was simply a matter of his getting back a lot more than he gave. Albert Schweitzer didn't consider his giving up careers in music, medicine, writing and teaching a sacrifice. He did that which was most important to him, that which gave him the most fulfillment. What he gave up was not important compared to the fulfillment he received while providing service to others.[29]

Discussion

1. Discuss what Tillich tells us that humankind had to mature sufficiently in order to understand Jesus as the Christ. How does the Old Testament contribute to this maturity?

2. What does Tillich mean when he says that Christianity is "the universal" center of history? Do you agree with his reasoning? What about other religions?

3. Do you agree that there are two principle functions of the church as described by Tillich? Can a church be the "true" representative of

---

29. Norman Cousins, *Albert Schweitzer's Mission: Healing and Peace* (New York: W.W. Norton, 1985).

Christ if one or the other function predominates over the other in an individual church?

4. Describe what is meant by a latent church. What do you think Tillich means when he tells us that the Christian church would not be able to represent the Kingdom of God without it?

5. Identify and discuss ways that the church has reformed itself in the past century or so.

6. Do you believe that the church is subject to demonization? If you agree, identify some demonization processes within the church that you know best. How does one tell the holy from the demonic?

7. Tillich tells us that a church must judge itself before it can rightfully judge events in the world? How does this judgment take place? How do you reconcile different judgements by different churches of the same event?

8. How has the church changed the climate of social relations through the years? How does this fit in with the reputation, deserved or undeserved, that the church represents the status quo of cultural norms?

9. Do you agree that the church must be a pacifist body? If you do, how can the outcome of a war be a significant occurrence in the Kingdom of God?

10. Do you agree that democracy has a special place in the Kingdom of God? If you do, how do you justify the weakness of many democracy in the world today?

11. Why does Tillich use the word "sacrifice" when he talks about an individuals involvement in the Kingdom? What does the word "sacrifice" mean to you? Do think it is necessary to sacrifice in order to be a Christian?

CHAPTER 9

The Kingdom Of God And The End Of History

Chapter Introduction

According to Tillich, the end of history will usher in the full Kingdom of God which, up until this time, has resided exclusively within the spirit of those who are part of the Spiritual Community. When the Kingdom arrives it will include everything positive that has been developed within an individual person as a part of eternity and Eternal Life. That which is negative will be purged.

Tillich's view of the end of history varies from that held by many church groups today. He does not believe in a heaven or hell, a judgement day, hell fire and damnation, a purgatory or a re-incarnation, as these symbols are not consistent with a loving God as witnessed through the life and death of Jesus the Christ.

Three points standout in this chapter:

1. It is God's wish that "all living things" develop their potential to the maximum degree possible. In regard to humans, however, development will preserve the individual's freedom of choice. As people develop as God desires, they will be in a constant state of renewal, becoming a New Being in Christ.

2. Eternal Life begins with this life, today, tomorrow and into the future. When an individual enters the Kingdom of God, the person's individuality is maintained and the process of development continues. The negatives acquired in life are purged but not forgotten.

3. Within Eternal Life all ambiguities are resolved through the unity provided by God's love.

The End of History: Eternal Life

The "end of history" and the abolishment of time—The arrival of the Kingdom of God may be regarded as "the end of history," according to Tillich. The world will have reached its aim. Time as currently understood will be abolished and replaced by "Eternal Life." When questions concerning the nature of eternal life are asked, according to Tillich, there are three possible answers: (1) a simple refusal to answer, (2) a supernatural response, and (3), the one preferred by Tillich, an interpretation of the symbol Kingdom of God.

A simple refusal to answer arises from the idea that Eternal Life is meant to be an unapproachable mystery, a mystery of the divine glory. Tillich has problems with this, as he believes that theology is meant to explore mysteries, including those of Eternal Life.

A supernatural response is just the opposite. It projects life—as it is experienced in this world—into the next world, after removing evil and estrangement. Hopes and dreams produced within the ambiguity and discord of the present life are projected forward and somehow fulfilled. It is primarily a matter of one's having the opportunity to decide "for salvation."

Tillich favors an interpretation of the symbol, Kingdom of God, which affirms that the ever-present aim of history is the elevation of the positive things that have happened within the world. At the same time, the negative elements which entangled the world are excluded. Tillich admits that this interpretation appears quite similar to the supernatural approach. He sees a critically important difference, however. In his interpretation of the Kingdom of God, every facet of life, in every moment of time, becomes a part of the Kingdom of God and Eternal Life. What happens in time or space, in the smallest particle of matter, as well as in the greatest personality, is significant to Eternal Life and the Kingdom of God, it is not simply a matter of personal salvation.

The ultimate judgment—The continuation of what is positive into Eternal Life presumes the elimination of an individual's negative, even including that which is intertwined and hidden by the good. In the New Testament Matthew tells us:

> *God will separate the chaff from the grain, burning the chaff with never ending fire, and storing away the grain. (Matthew 3:12)*

In Tillich's view, there is no judgement that sorts out individuals, one who is 51% good going to "heaven," and the other, who is only 49% good, going to "hell." All that is good within all individuals goes to "heaven."

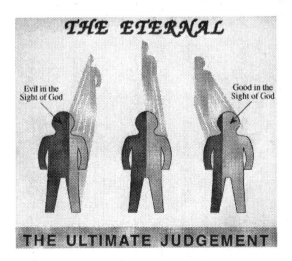

Tillich suggests that there is a continuous process as a person moves from the reality of existence to the eternal. Eternity begins in this life and is characterized by one's eternal memory, which includes the past, present as well as the future. He suggests that not much more than this can be said about eternity—except through poetry or other forms of aesthetic expression. But the little that can be said has important consequences for understanding eternity. The eternal is not a future state of things. It is the past, the present, and the future—it is always present, not only in humans, but also in everything that has being.

There are some people who believe that eternity is a return to a state of mere potentiality. This includes the removal of everything gained within life, positive as well as negative. According to Tillich, this idea is more adequate to the India-born religions than to any of those that are Israel-born. In this view the whole world process produces nothing, which Tillich does not accept.

The end of history and the final conquest—Eternal Life is identical with the fulfillment of the Kingdom of God and the elimination of all the problems and ambiguities one faces in life. Tillich illustrates this point by showing how certain situations that are ambiguous in life are no longer so in Eternal Life.

In Eternal Life, as an example, the opposites, individualization and community, are perfectly united in divine love. In the opposites, dynamics and form (stability), the divine creativity transcends the difference in a way that preserves the stability of the individual. In the opposites, freedom and destiny, there is perfect unity between the two as they are transcended by a divine freedom that is identical to a divine destiny. Tillich, as he briefly touches on these changes in relationships between opposites, notes that the divine resolves the problems of opposites by transcending the individual self. At the same time, the individual essence of each person is preserved. The continuation of one's individual self into Eternal Life is an important Christian belief not held by Eastern religions.

Tillich now turns to the three functions of the spirit: morality, culture, and religion, and their relationship to Eternal Life. According to Tillich, within Eternal Life all three functions of the spirit end as special functions. In respect to *morality* there is no longer an ought-to-be, as it has been achieved; no law is necessary, as the love experienced in Eternal Life does what the law demands before it is demanded. In respect to *culture*, there is no "truth" that is not already done, and there is no aesthetic expression that is not also a reality in Eternal Life. In respect to *religion*, which is necessary to counter the estrangement of an alienated world, there is no estrangement or alienation, there is total blessedness.

Eternal blessedness—According to many theologians, when one arrives at a state of blessedness (becomes holy) in Eternal Life, the divine Spirit produces a feeling of fulfillment that cannot be disrupted. Within one's secular existence, however, the blessed remain aware of the negatives in life such as despair, unhappiness, and condemnation.

It is often observed, according to Tillich, that a life or a state of blessedness is difficult to imagine without at least some degree of negativity within it, although less so as one becomes increasingly blessed. A major problem associated with acquiring blessedness is that it appears that negatives are necessary in the development of one's blessedness. This appears to conflict with the position that the negative within a person is eliminated and does not become a part of the Kingdom of God and Eternal Life.

Some philosophers and theologians resolve this problem by suggesting that God, as parent, suffered in the suffering of the Christ. Through such an experience, negatives necessary for the development of blessedness are present within the divine. Many theologians and churches, however, reject this idea as it would bring God down to the level of the passionate and suffering gods of Greek mythology. According to Tillich, present day theology—with few exceptions—avoids this question entirely, either by ignoring it or calling it a divine mystery. As far as Tillich is concerned, if theology refuses to answer such important questions, it has neglected its task.

As Tillich sees it, theology must take seriously the philosophers and theologians who propose a suffering God even though that presumes a negative element in Eternal Life. Tillich, as do many others (particularly in the field of psychology), suggests that the development of blessedness requires a negative element. Given this, Tillich believes that blessedness is not some absolute state of perpetual perfection. The divine Life of blessedness is dynamic, it is understanding, it cannot be disturbed by the negatives of life, even though having experienced them. It is analogous to the temptations (Matthew 4:1-11), that were experienced by Jesus, although he did not succumb to them.

The Individual and Eternal Destiny

Individual and universal fulfillment—Tillich has been addressing Eternal Life and its application to earthly life. He now addresses the functioning of the human spirit. He does this because humans are able to effect their own destiny as no other living thing is able to do.

Only humans are aware of the elements of "ought-to-be," of responsibility, guilt, despair, and hope. This awareness provides humans the unique opportunity to turn toward God. Humans alone, as individuals, have the freedom to decide whether they will develop the potentialities given to them by God or waste them. Humans can fulfill the potentialities, though not totally; and they can waste their potentialities, but not completely. Possibly, one may include so much negative in one's life that essentially all of one's innate potentiality has been wasted, leaving very little positive for Eternal Life. One can elevate oneself to greatness, or reduce oneself to smallness. These are relative terms. Obviously many gradations of greatness and smallness lie between these extremes. According to Tillich, this relativity contradicts the possibility of an absolute judgment that appears in religious symbolism such as "being saved" or "being lost," "eternal life" or "eternal death," "heaven" or "hell." The idea of "eternal death" destroys even the positive within the individual: even though it may be small and insignificant, it is an expression of God's being.

Tillich introduces the idea of "essentialization" as an alternative to absolute judgment, essentialization being the process involved in developing one's potentiality. He includes within this concept the assurance of elevating the positive into eternity even in the most unfulfilled life. At the same time, he emphasizes the despair of having wasted one's potentialities.

An absolute judgment involving a two-part eternal destiny for individuals—eternal life or eternal death—contradicts God's act of creation described in Genesis, 1:31: "God saw all God had made, and indeed it was very good." According to Tillich, if being, as being, is good, nothing that exists can become completely evil. Tillich believes strongly in what he calls "the doctrine of the unity of everything in divine love" as it exists in the Kingdom of God. This doctrine deprives the symbol "hell" of its character as "eternal damnation." It does not take away the seriousness of the condemning side of the divine judgment, and the despair in which the negative is experienced. It does remove the literal folly of a heaven and hell.

Another side of human nature also contradicts an absolute "heaven" or "hell" doctrine. The total person, including one's conscious and unconscious sides, is largely decided by the social conditions one is subjected to upon birth. Individuals grow interdependently with the social conditions surrounding them. Freedom to act, in spite of social conditions, and the freedom to act as influenced by social conditions, are inseparable from each other and are present within all individuals.

Consequently, to separate the judgment of an individual from that of all society is not just.

Only the essentialization and elevation of all that is positive into Eternal Life responds to the questions concerning distorted forms of life, forms that, because of physical, biological, psychological, or sociological conditions are unable to develop their potential (including those who prematurely die). Whoever condemns anyone to eternal death condemns themselves, because one's individual self cannot be separated from all others.

The meaning of resurrection—According to Tillich, rather than using the symbol "immortality" to describe humanity's taking part in Eternal Life beyond death, it is better expressed by the symbol "resurrection of the body." Even then, he much prefers the symbol used by the Apostle Paul, "resurrection of the spiritual body":

> ...*it is sown a physical body, it is raised a spiritual body. If there is a physical body, there is a spiritual body. (I Corinthians 15:44)*

The Spiritual Body, according to the Apostle Paul, results from God's invading, transforming and elevating an individual's spirit beyond itself. A Spiritual Body then is a body that expresses the spiritually transformed personality of the individual. Tillich suggests that only poetic and artistic imagination can take one's understanding beyond this point.

The Christian emphasis on resurrection also includes an affirmation that one participates in the Kingdom of God as an individual. Does one maintain one's individuality in Eternal Life? Tillich believes that the individual self cannot be excluded from Eternal Life; to do so is to deny God's purpose for humans, the full development of one's potential.

Another point that Tillich makes about the presence of the individual self in Eternal Life concerns the nature of that self. It does not remain unchanging in some form of static stupor—this denies the function of individual self-consciousness, reflection, and change. The self-conscious self in Eternal Life is not what it is in existing life.

The symbol, resurrection, is often used to express the certainty of Eternal Life after death. When used in this sense it symbolically represents the idea of the New Being. The New Being is the transformation of the old being rather than the creation of a new being, per se. This is the universal hope.

Eternal life and death—Tillich begins by asserting that everything created is rooted in God, the "ground of our being," and as such, is a product of God. If this is true, non-being, or death, cannot prevail. He then raises the question: How can the ideas of Eternal Life and eternal death be united? How can we reconcile the seriousness of death with the truth that everything comes from eternity and must return to it? The history of Christian thought reveals two powerfully represented sides.

The first side, which emphasizes the death of those not saved, is predominant in the teaching and preaching of many churches today; in many of them it has become official doctrine. The second side asserts that we belong to eternity and we will return from our existing lives to eternity because we are created by God who is eternal. This is true, even though we turn away from God. According to Tillich, this second side is the predominant view in mystical and humanistic movements within churches and sects. The controversies rage between these two viewpoints. They involve heated theological discussions on the very nature of God, humanity, and the relationship between the two and the discussion has considerable psychological as well as theological significance.

Tillich, in responding to this, begins by discussing the motives underlying one or the other position. The threat-of-death position belongs to the ethical-educational type of thinking found in many churches. This type of thinking fears that a belief in the universal salvation of all beings would undermine or perhaps destroy the seriousness of religious and ethical decisions. As far as Tillich is concerned, this fear has some foundation and we should not ignore it.

Tillich then goes on to discuss the differences between beliefs within and outside of Christianity. He addresses three possibilities: (1) the idea of reincarnation, (2) the idea of purgatory, and (3) the idea of an intermediate state (limbo). All three of these beliefs express the idea that the moment of death is the decisive moment that decides whether one has Eternal Life or eternal death. This idea is nonsense, according to Tillich, when considering the death of infants, children, or underdeveloped adults. Even in instances of adult maturity it ignores the presence of social influences on the person, as well as the continuing process of "essentialization" cut short by early death. This is not God's justice.

Regarding the reincarnation of individual life, Tillich recognizes that it has great power over many millions of Asiatic people. As far as he is concerned, however, reincarnation does not answer the question of how to find a middle ground between Eternal Life and eternal death. Furthermore, Hinduism and Buddhism, the proponents of re-incarnation, do not believe that the individual self is maintained within the eternal. Within the re-incarnation experience, there is the difficulty of trying to experience an individual's personal identity from one reincarnation experience to the next. There is no conscious memory between existences.

Purgatory is a state in which the soul is "purged" from the sin that has corrupted it during one's secular life. In Catholic doctrine, it is the suffering in purgatory that cleanses the soul from the sinfulness of one's past life. Besides the psychological impossibility of imagining uninterrupted periods of mere suffering, it is a theological mistake, according to Tillich, to derive the transformation to blessedness strictly from pain alone instead of from God's love.

The doctrine of limbo, or the intermediary state between death and resurrection, was Protestantism's rejection of the idea of purgatory.

This was due principally to the abuse of the purgatory idea through the selling of indulgences as a means of shortening the time spent there. According to Tillich, the Protestant attempt was a rather weak one, involving the idea of a bodiless intermediary state and is not worthy of further consideration.

None of these three symbols are satisfactory. According to Tillich, a more adequate answer than any of the above involves an Eternal Life that evolves toward a greater qualitative fulfillment. Within this idea, one's positive existing life is included. Eternity does not maintain an individual's identity as a static, unchanging presence, nor does it subject an individual to constant change; both are contained within the eternal unity of the divine Life. One's individual destiny comes about through the destiny of the entire universe. The Catholic doctrine of prayer and sacrifice for the dead is a powerful expression of this thinking.

Tillich tells us that it is obvious, given what has been said above, that the symbols heaven and hell need not be included within theological thought. If they have value, it is as symbols, not actual places. As symbols they express states of blessedness and despair, and are valuable only if used in this sense. When thought of literally, they are frequently accompanied by evil psychological effects. Psychology can only address the neurotic consequences of the literal distortion of heaven and hell. This would be needed less if the church's preaching and teaching would remove the superstitious implications of their literal use.

The Kingdom of God: Time and Eternity

Eternal Life and divine life—God is eternal and is subjected to neither the processes, limits, or structure within which humans exist. God, as eternal, retains a specific identity and, simultaneously, is involved in ever greater perfect fulfillment.

According to Tillich, the eternal God who is also the living God, is referred to in the New Testament as the Eternal One. In other words,

Eternal Life is lived only in God. Eternal Life "in" God suggests three possibilities. It suggests the presence of all potentiality, and all creativity possible, in the divine mind of God. It suggests the dependence of all life (even when in a state of estrangement and despair) on the eternal God. And it points to the presence of one's individual fulfillment within God's ultimate fulfillment.

According to Tillich, this threefold "in-ness" shows the rhythm of one's individual life with God. It is the process of beginning with one's potential, the separation from God into estrangement, finally culminating in a personal fulfillment in God that moves beyond one's original potential. Tillich tells us that God's act of creation is spurred by love that finds fulfillment only through individual lives that have the freedom to accept or reject this love. God desires the actualization and essentialization of everything that has being, including humans.

Commentary

C.S. Lewis (author of more than 30 books and a specialist in Renaissance literature as a professor at Cambridge University), provides some helpful insights into the nature of "heaven" in his book, *The Great Divorce*. God and a new arrival in heaven are watching a procession of boys and girls, hand in hand, singing and paying honor to a lady within their midst. God is asked:

> *"And who are all these young men and women on each side?"*
> *"They are her sons and daughters".*
> *"She must have had a very large family."*
> *"Every young man or boy that met her became her son—even if it was only the boy that brought the*
> *meat to her back door. Every girl that met her was her daughter."*
> *"Isn't that a bit hard on their own parents?"*

"No. There are those that steal other people's children. But her mother-
hood was of a different kind. Those on whom it fell went back to their natural parents loving them more. Few men looked on her without becoming,
in a certain fashion, her lovers. But it was the kind of love that made them
not less true, but truer, to their own wives."

"And how... but hullo! What are all these animals. A cat—two cats—
dozens of cats. And all those dogs...why, I can't count them. And the birds.
And the horses."

"They are her beasts."

"Did she keep a sort of zoo? I mean, this is a bit too much."

"Every beast and bird that came near her had its place in her love. In
her they became themselves. And now the abundance of life she has in
Christ from the Father/Mother flows over them."[30]

Discussion

1. What do you think Tillich means when he says that every facet of
   life, in every moment of time, becomes a part of the Kingdom of
   God?

2. How do you perceive heaven and hell? The final judgement?

3. Do you agree that nothing that is good is destroyed? How might this
   be reconciled with the presence of the negative if all that was created
   was good?

4. Do you agree that some negative is essential to the development of
   blessedness? Why?

---

30. C.S. Lewis, *The Great Divorce* (New York: Macmillan Publishing Company, Inc.
1946), pp 80-82.

5. What is the New Being? How does it differ, or does it, from the divine Spirit or Jesus?

   How does the symbol resurrection, when it stands for Eternal Life, represent the idea of a New Being?

6. Why do you think other religions do not include the preservation of the individual identity through eternity?

7. Do you accept Tillich's ideas on re-incarnation, purgatory and limbo? Why?

8. What does Tillich mean when he says "in God?"